Access 2013:
Basic

Student Manual

MOS Edition

Access 2013: Basic

Chief Executive Officer, Axzo Press:	Ken Wasnock
Series Designer and COO:	Adam A. Wilcox
Vice President, Operations:	Josh Pincus
Director of Publishing Systems Development:	Dan Quackenbush
Writer:	Steve English
Keytester:	Cliff Coryea

Trademarks

Disclaimer

We reserve the right to revise this publication and make changes from time to time in its content without notice.

ISBN 10: 1-4260-3613-2
ISBN 13: 978-1-4260-3613-2

Printed in the United States of America

1 2 3 4 5 GL 06 05 04 03

Contents

Introduction

After reading this introduction, you will know how to:

A Use ILT Series manuals in general.

B Use prerequisites, a target student description, course objectives, and a skills inventory to properly set your expectations for the course.

C Re-key this course after class.

Topic A: About the manual

ILT Series philosophy

Our manuals facilitate your learning by providing structured interaction with the software itself. While we provide text to explain difficult concepts, the hands-on activities are the focus of our courses. By paying close attention as your instructor leads you through these activities, you will learn the skills and concepts effectively.

We believe strongly in the instructor-led class. During class, focus on your instructor. Our manuals are designed and written to facilitate your interaction with your instructor, and not to call attention to manuals themselves.

We believe in the basic approach of setting expectations, delivering instruction, and providing summary and review afterwards. For this reason, lessons begin with objectives and end with summaries. We also provide overall course objectives and a course summary to provide both an introduction to and closure on the entire course.

Manual components

The manuals contain these major components:

- Table of contents
- Introduction
- Units
- Course summary
- Glossary
- Index

Each element is described below.

Table of contents

The table of contents acts as a learning roadmap.

Introduction

The introduction contains information about our training philosophy and our manual components, features, and conventions. It contains target student, prerequisite, objective, and setup information for the specific course.

Units

Units are the largest structural component of the course content. A unit begins with a title page that lists objectives for each major subdivision, or topic, within the unit. Within each topic, conceptual and explanatory information alternates with hands-on activities. Units conclude with a summary comprising one paragraph for each topic, and an independent practice activity that gives you an opportunity to practice the skills you've learned.

The conceptual information takes the form of text paragraphs, exhibits, lists, and tables. The activities are structured in two columns, one telling you what to do, the other providing explanations, descriptions, and graphics.

Course summary

This section provides a text summary of the entire course. It is useful for providing closure at the end of the course. The course summary also indicates the next course in this series, if there is one, and lists additional resources you might find useful as you continue to learn about the software.

Glossary

The glossary provides definitions for all of the key terms used in this course.

Index

The index at the end of this manual makes it easy for you to find information about a particular software component, feature, or concept.

Manual conventions

We've tried to keep the number of elements and the types of formatting to a minimum in the manuals. This aids in clarity and makes the manuals more classically elegant looking. But there are some conventions and icons you should know about.

Item	Description
Italic text	In conceptual text, indicates a new term or feature.
Bold text	In unit summaries, indicates a key term or concept. In an independent practice activity, indicates an explicit item that you select, choose, or type.
`Code font`	Indicates code or syntax.
`Longer strings of ▶ code will look ▶ like this.`	In the hands-on activities, any code that's too long to fit on a single line is divided into segments by one or more continuation characters (▶). This code should be entered as a continuous string of text.
Select **bold item**	In the left column of hands-on activities, bold sans-serif text indicates an explicit item that you select, choose, or type.
Keycaps like (↵ ENTER)	Indicate a key on the keyboard you must press.

Hands-on activities

The hands-on activities are the most important parts of our manuals. They are divided into two primary columns. The "Here's how" column gives short instructions to you about what to do. The "Here's why" column provides explanations, graphics, and clarifications. Here's a sample:

Do it!

A-1:   Creating a commission formula

Here's how	Here's why
1 Open Sales	This is an oversimplified sales compensation worksheet. It shows sales totals, commissions, and incentives for five sales reps.
2 Observe the contents of cell F4	F4 ▼ ☐ = =E4*C_Rate The commission rate formulas use the name "C_Rate" instead of a value for the commission rate.

For these activities, we have provided a collection of data files designed to help you learn each skill in a real-world business context. As you work through the activities, you will modify and update these files. Of course, you might make a mistake and therefore want to re-key the activity starting from scratch. To make it easy to start over, you will rename each data file at the end of the first activity in which the file is modified. Our convention for renaming files is to add the word "My" to the beginning of the file name. In the above activity, for example, a file called "Sales" is being used for the first time. At the end of this activity, you would save the file as "My sales," thus leaving the "Sales" file unchanged. If you make a mistake, you can start over using the original "Sales" file.

In some activities, however, it might not be practical to rename the data file. If you want to retry one of these activities, ask your instructor for a fresh copy of the original data file.

Topic B: Setting your expectations

Properly setting your expectations is essential to your success. This topic will help you do that by providing:

- Prerequisites for this course
- A description of the target student
- A list of the objectives for the course
- A skills assessment for the course

Course prerequisites

Before taking this course, you should be familiar with personal computers and the use of a keyboard and a mouse. Furthermore, this course assumes that you have completed the following course or have equivalent experience:

- *Windows 7: Basic, Windows Vista: Basic,* or *Windows XP: Basic*

Target student

You should be comfortable using a personal computer and Microsoft Windows. You will get the most out of this course if your goal is to become proficient in creating database tables, queries, forms, and reports, and in sorting and filtering data in Access.

Course objectives

These overall course objectives will give you an idea about what to expect from the course. It is also possible that they will help you see that this course is not the right one for you. If you think you either lack the prerequisite knowledge or already know most of the subject matter to be covered, you should let your instructor know that you think you are misplaced in the class.

Note: In addition to the general objectives listed below, specific Microsoft Office Specialist exam objectives are listed at the beginning of each topic (where applicable).

After completing this course, you will know how to:

- Organize data efficiently by using a database management system; start Access, open Access databases and identify components of the Access window.
- Plan and create a database; use Datasheet view and Design view; create, modify, and work in tables; and set the primary key for a table.
- Modify a table's design; use the Attachment data type; find and replace values; and sort, filter, and delete records.
- Set field properties; create input masks; and set validation rules.
- Create queries, and sort and filter the results; modify queries; and perform operations in queries.
- Create, modify, and work with forms; and use them to sort and filter records.
- Create, modify, and print reports; and add summary fields to a report.

Skills inventory

Use the following form to gauge your skill level entering the class. For each skill listed, rate your familiarity from 1 to 5, with five being the most familiar. *This is not a test.* Rather, it is intended to provide you with an idea of where you're starting from at the beginning of class. If you're wholly unfamiliar with all the skills, you might not be ready for the class. If you think you already understand all of the skills, you might need to move on to the next course in the series. In either case, you should let your instructor know as soon as possible.

Skill	1	2	3	4	5
Identifying database components					
Starting and examining Access					
Opening a database					
Examining the Database window and a database table					
Planning and creating a database					
Examining a table in Datasheet view and Design view					
Creating a table by using a template and Design view					
Adding fields to a table and setting the primary key					
Saving and adding records					
Modifying field names and deleting and inserting fields					
Finding and replacing values in a table					
Sorting records					
Filtering records					
Setting field properties					
Creating an input mask					
Setting validation rules					
Creating queries by using the Query Wizard and Design view					
Sorting and filtering query results					
Adding fields to and removing fields from a query					
Using comparison operators and calculations in a query					

Skill	1	2	3	4	5
Creating and modifying forms					
Sorting and filtering records in a form					
Creating reports					
Grouping and summarizing data in a report					
Printing a report					

Topic C: Re-keying the course

If you have the proper hardware and software, you can re-key this course after class. This section explains what you'll need in order to do so and how to do it.

Hardware requirements

Your personal computer should have:

- A keyboard and a mouse
- 1 GHz processor (or faster)
- 1 GB RAM (or higher)
- 2 GB of available hard drive space after operating system install
- CD-ROM drive
- A monitor with at least 1024 × 768 resolution

Software requirements

You will also need the following software:

- Microsoft Windows 7
- Microsoft Office 2013 (minimally, you can install only Access)

Network requirements

The following network components and connectivity are also required for re-keying this course:

- Internet access, for the following purposes:
  - Updating the Windows operating system and Microsoft Office 2013
  - Opening Help files at Microsoft Office Online (If online Help is not available, you will not be able to complete Activity C-1 in the unit titled "Getting started.")

Setup instructions to re-key the course

Before you re-key the course, you will need to set up your computer.

1 Install Windows 7 on an NTFS partition according to the software publisher's instructions. After installation is complete, if your machine has Internet access, use Windows Update to install any critical updates and service packs.

   Note: You can also use Windows Vista or Windows XP, but the screenshots in this course were taken in Windows 7, so your screens will look different.

2 With flat-panel displays, we recommend using the panel's native resolution for best results. Color depth/quality should be set to High (24 bit) or higher.

3   Install Microsoft Office 2013 according to the software manufacturer's
    instructions, as follows:
    a   When prompted for the CD key, enter the code included with your
        software.
    b   Select "Customize installation" and click Next.
    c   Click the Installation Options tab.
    d   For Microsoft Office Access, Office Shared Features, and Office Tools,
        click the down-arrow and choose "Run all from My Computer."
    e   Set all *except* the following to Not Available: Microsoft Office Access,
        Office Shared Features, and Office Tools.
    f   Click Install Now.

4   Update Microsoft Office 2013 as follows:
    a   Open Windows Update. Under "Get updates for other Microsoft
        products", click "Find out more."
    b   Check "I agree to the Terms of Use for Microsoft Update" and click
        Next.
    c   Choose "Use recommended settings" and click Install.".

5   If you have the data disc that came with this manual, locate the Student Data
    folder on it and copy it to your Windows desktop.

    If you don't have the data disc, you can download the Student Data files for the
    course:
    a   Connect to http://downloads.logicaloperations.com.
    b   Enter the course title or search by part to locate this course
    c   Click the course title to display a list of available downloads.
        Note: Data Files are located under the Instructor Edition of the course.
    d   Click the link(s) for downloading the Student Data files.
    e   Create a folder named Student Data on the desktop of your computer.
    f   Double-click the downloaded zip file(s) and drag the contents into the
        Student Data folder.

6   Start Microsoft Office Access 2013. Then do the following:
    a   Activate the software and click Finish.
    b   Start Access 2013.
    c   Click Blank desktop database. The Blank desktop database dialog box
        opens.
    d   Click the browse button and navigate to the Topic A folder in the Unit 1
        folder in the Student Data folder.
    e   Give the database a filename of Database1, and click OK.
    f   Click Create to open the database.
    g   On the File tab, click Options. In the Access Options dialog box, click
        Trust Center and then click Trust Center Settings. In the Trust Center
        dialog box, click Macro Settings and select Enable All Macros. This will
        prevent a security warning from appearing every time you open a database
        file. Click OK twice to close the dialog boxes.
    h   Close Access.

Unit 1

Getting started

Complete this unit, and you'll know how to:

A Organize data efficiently by using a
database management system.

B Start Access, learn about its environment,
open a database file with shared access,
and learn about database objects.

Topic A: Database concepts

Explanation

Microsoft Access 2013, a component of the Microsoft Office suite, is a database management program: an application that stores and organizes data and makes data retrieval efficient. A *database* is an organized collection of data, or information. An example of a simple database is a phone book that contains the names, phone numbers, and addresses of individuals and businesses.

Database components

The following table defines several database-related terms used in Access:

Term	Description
Data value	An item of data. In Exhibit 1-1, 2.25 is a data value.
Record	All of the data values that apply to a specific item listed in the table. In Exhibit 1-1, each row in the table is a record that contains all data for a single spice.
Field	A specific type of data that applies to each item listed in the table. In Exhibit 1-1, each column in the table is a field that contains data values for each spice. For example, Field 3 contains the price of each spice. The column heading can be the same as the field name, but it is often a more user-friendly and descriptive label.
Table	A collection of records. The records and fields in a table form its rows and columns. Exhibit 1-1 shows a simple table named tblProduct. It contains four fields and ten records.

Exhibit 1-1: The tblProduct table

Do it!   **A-1:   Identifying database components**

Here's how	Here's why
1 Observe the table shown in Exhibit 1-1	This table contains ten rows and four columns.
2 Observe the column headings	The headings are Product ID, Product Name, Unit Price, Amount, and Unit. Each column represents a field.
3 Observe the data values in each field	Each field contains a specific type of data value. The field corresponds to the columns.
4 Observe the rows	Each row contains data for a single product. For example, the fifth row contains the record for chamomile flowers. The records correspond to the rows.

Relational databases

Explanation

Microsoft Access creates *relational databases*, in which data is organized in related tables. In related tables, one or more fields are linked to fields in another table. This link ensures that you can enter only those values that have corresponding entries in the other table. For example, suppose that you store product details and sales details in two tables. These tables can be related by using the common field ProductID. This common field ensures that you cannot enter the sales details of any products that are not included in the product details table.

A relational database can have multiple tables that contain data about various entities, such as products, sales, or customers. An *entity* is any object that has a distinct set of properties. A relational database helps you store data in an orderly manner so that you can retrieve it efficiently. For example, if you need to display the product details and sales details in a single report, you can use the corresponding tables to get the information.

Related tables help reduce data redundancy. For instance, if you have a table of details about the products you sell and another table of sales transactions, the sales table need list only the ID numbers of the products sold; it doesn't need to list all of the product details.

Do it!

A-2:   Identifying the advantages of relational databases

Questions and answers
1 What is a relational database?
2 True or false? Microsoft Access is used to create relational databases.
3 What are the advantages of using a relational database?

Topic B: Exploring the Access environment

This topic covers the following Microsoft Office Specialist exam objectives for Access 2013.

#	Objective
1.3	**Navigate through a Database**
1.3.4	Set navigation options

Components of the Access window

Explanation

To start Access, click Start and choose All Programs, Microsoft Office 2013, Access 2013.

The opening Access screen, shown in Exhibit 1-2, offers a number of templates that can be used to create databases. Some templates are included with the application, while others have to be downloaded from the Internet. There are also options to create a new blank database, open a recently used database, and sign in to a Microsoft account.

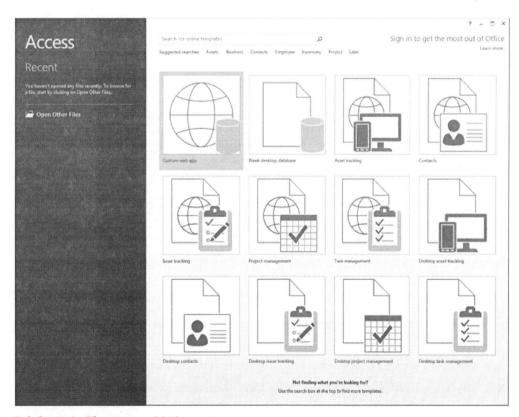

Exhibit 1-2: The Access 2013 opening screen

Most of your time, however, won't be spent looking at the opening screen; it will be spent working on databases via the user interface.

Do it!

B-1: Starting Access

Here's how	Here's why
1 Click **Start** and choose **All Programs**, **Microsoft Office 2013**, **Access 2013**	To start Access. The Microsoft Access window appears, as shown in Exhibit 1-2.
Maximize the window	If necessary.
2 Observe the list of Recent databases.	Your instructor created Database1 when installing Access 2013.
3 Click **Database1**	To open this blank database.
4 Click **File**	To display the File tab. The Info screen appears by default.
Observe the selections on the **File** tab	The file tab includes selections for saving, opening, and closing databases. It also includes a selection for signing in to a Microsoft account. The Options command appears at the bottom of the list.
5 Click **Options**	On the File tab. The File tab closes, Database 1 displays, and the Access Options dialog box opens.
Select various categories in the left pane and observe the settings that are available	Don't make any changes at this time.
6 Click **Cancel**	To close the Access Options dialog box.
7 Close the database	Click File, Close.

Opening databases

Explanation
To open a database, use the Office Backstage. To do this, click Open Other Files on the startup screen. From the Office Backstage, click the area from which you want to open a database:

Open Place	Description
Recent	By default, Access displays a list of your most recently opened files, along with their locations. Click a filename to reopen that file.
SkyDrive	Used to sign in to a Microsoft account, allowing you to open any of your database files that are located in Microsoft's SkyDrive cloud storage.
Computer	Used to open files located in folders on hard drives in your local computer.
Add a Place	Used to create cloud storage locations on Office 365 Sharepoint or on SkyDrive.

File formats

When you open or create a database, its file format appears in parentheses after the database name in the title bar. The *file format* is the specific format in which each application stores data. By default, Access 2013 creates databases in the .accdb file format first introduced in Access 2007. A database created in the current Access file format typically cannot be opened in Access 2003 or earlier versions of Access, but Access 2013 can work with earlier formats. For backward compatibility, files can be saved in Access 2002–2003 format or in Access 2000 format.

Shared access

When you open a database file, it opens with *shared access* by default. This means that while you are editing and changing the database, other users can open and edit it at the same time.

The Ribbon

Access 2013 uses a ribbon interface, shown in Exhibit 1-3, to display commands and options. The ribbon is divided into tabs, each of which contains a related group of commands and icons. These are context sensitive—they change depending on what kind of object (table, form, query, or report) is open, and in what view. Also, the more screen space the Access window has, the more ribbon commands and text will be shown.

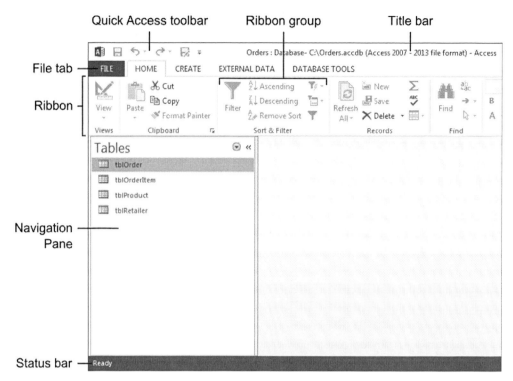

Exhibit 1-3: An open database and the ribbon

The following table describes the components of the Access window:

Item	Description
File tab	The File tab contains commands for creating, opening, saving, and publishing databases, saving database objects, printing data, and exiting the program. The File tab also contains the Options command, which opens the Access Options dialog box.
Quick Access toolbar	Contains icons for frequently used commands, such as Save, Print, and Undo. You can customize it to add other commands.
Title bar	Displays the name and file format of the current database.
Ribbon group	Contains menus, commands, lists, and galleries.
Ribbon	Contains tabs that are divided into groups.
Navigation Pane	Lists tables, queries, forms, reports, and other database objects. To show different objects, use the drop-down menu at the top of the pane. Click the double arrow in the pane's upper-right corner to expand and collapse the pane.
Status bar	Displays status messages, View buttons, and the document zoom slider when a table, query, report, or other database object is open.

Do it!   **B-2:   Opening a database**

The files for this activity are in Student Data folder **Unit 1\Topic B**.

Here's how	Here's why
1 Click **File**	
Click **Open**	To display the Open page.
Click **Computer**	You'll open a database file on your computer.
Click **Browse**	To display the Open dialog box.
2 Navigate to the current topic folder within the Student Data folder	To display the files in the current topic folder.
Select **Orders**	(If necessary.) You'll open this database.
Click **Open**	
3 Observe the Access title bar	The title bar displays "Orders : Database." This is followed by the file path, and then by "(Access 2007 – 2013 file format)." Access 2013 uses the file format established in Access 2007.
4 Observe the ribbon	It has tabs for various categories of commands. Related commands on each tab are placed together in groups.

Navigating a database

Explanation

When a database opens, its name and format appear in the title bar, and the Navigation Pane opens on the left side of the Access window, as shown in Exhibit 1-3.

The Navigation Pane displays the objects in your database. Objects include tables, forms, queries, and reports. You can use the Navigation Pane to change which objects are displayed and in what order. For instance, you can display just tables, or all objects (see Exhibit 1-4).

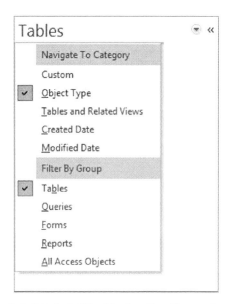

Exhibit 1-4: The Navigation Pane, showing the drop-down menu

Access database objects

The following table describes objects used in Access databases:

Object	Description
Table	Stores data. For example, you can use a table to store details about employees, such as name, title, and department.
Query	Retrieves specific information—such as which product had the highest sales for a given month, or which employees work in the Western region—from a table.
Form	Used to enter data into a database table. You can also use a form to view and modify records in a table.
Report	Prints or displays data. You can customize a report by applying different font styles and headings.
Macro	Automates frequently performed database tasks, such as printing a set of weekly reports.
Module	Automates and customizes database operations. Modules are programs written in Visual Basic.

Navigation options

You can use the Navigation Options dialog box, shown in Exhibit 1-5, to change the look and behavior of the Navigation Pane. For instance, you can have objects open with a single click, and you can show hidden and system objects. To open this dialog box, right-click the title bar or a blank area of the Navigation Pane and choose Navigation Options.

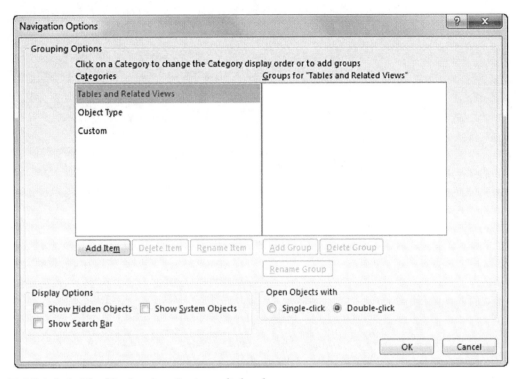

Exhibit 1-5: The Navigation Options dialog box

B-3: Using the Navigation Pane

Here's how	Here's why
1 Observe the Navigation Pane	(On the left side of the window.) It shows the tables in the database. Tables, reports, forms, and other items in Access are called *objects*.
2 In the Navigation Pane, click **Tables**	You'll see the drop-down menu shown in Exhibit 1-4. Here you can select which objects are displayed in the pane.
Choose **All Access Objects**	All objects appear in the Navigation Pane, and the top of the pane now says "All Access Objects." In addition to the tables, you see a query and a report.
3 Click **All Access Objects** and choose **Modified Date**	All of the objects appear in the order of modification, with the latest at the top.
4 Click **All Dates**	The drop-down menu now says "All Dates" to indicate that the objects are ordered by date.
Observe the menu	It now shows options for specifying which objects to show based on how old they are.
5 Show only tables in the Navigation Pane	Use the menu to choose Object Type and then Tables.
6 In the upper-right corner of the Navigation Pane, click «	To collapse the pane and give you more room to work.
Expand the pane	Click the double arrow.
7 Right-click a blank area of the Navigation Pane and choose **Navigation Options...**	To open the Navigation Options dialog box
Observe the options you can set	You can show hidden objects, change the order in which categories are displayed, add groups, and have objects open with a single click.
8 Click **Cancel**	To close the dialog box without making any changes.

Opening a database table

Explanation

You open a table to view and edit its contents. To open any database object, double-click its name in the Navigation Pane. Double-clicking a table will open it in Datasheet view, as opposed to Design view or any other view that might be available. You can also right-click a table and choose Open from the shortcut menu.

If you open multiple tables or other objects, Access 2013 displays them as a series of tabbed documents. You can change this default to hide all but the active object.

Do it!

B-4:   Examining a database table

Here's how	Here's why
1 In the Navigation Pane, double-click **tblProduct**	To show the contents of this table.
2 Observe the headings in the Table window	The table has five fields. The field headings are Product ID, Product Name, Unit Price, Amount, and Unit.
3 Observe the rows and columns in the table	Each row corresponds to a record, and each column corresponds to a field.
4 Right-click the **tblProduct** tab and choose **Close**	To close the table. You can also click the Close button (X) in the upper-right corner of the table. (Don't click the X in the upper-right corner of the Access window; that would close Access.)
5 Click the **File** tab and choose **Close**	To close the database.

Unit summary: Getting started

Topic A In this topic, you learned that a **database** stores data in the form of tables. You learned that a table contains records and fields. You also learned about **relational databases**, which store data in related tables.

Topic B In this topic, you learned how to start Access and you examined the **Microsoft Access** window. You learned about the **Navigation Pane**, which is used to specify which database objects you see, and in what order. You also learned how to open a database file with **shared access**.

Review questions

1 Identify the correct term for each of the following:

Description	Term
A set of related data values	
A collection of records	
An item of data	

2 Let's say you're working with a database that contains information about the salespeople at Outlander Spices. Which object would you use for each of the following tasks?

Task	Database object
Enter information for a new salesperson.	
Find departments with earnings of more than $80,000.	
Print all values from the table.	

3 What is a relational database?

4 Name two sources used by the Help system.

5 What is shared access?

Independent practice activity

In this activity, you'll identify Access components, open a database and identify database objects, and open a table. Then you'll close the table and the database.

The files for this activity are in Student Data folder **Unit 1\Unit summary**.

1 Open OrdersIPA.

2 In the Access window, identify the Navigation Pane.

3 Identify the types and number of database objects in the database. (*Hint:* Choose All Access Objects from the Navigation Pane menu.)

4 Open the tblEmployee table. How many fields and records are there in this table?

5 Close the tblEmployee table.

6 Close the OrdersIPA database.

Unit 2

Databases and tables

Complete this unit, and you'll know how to:

A Plan and create a database.

B Examine a table in Datasheet view and Design view.

C Create and modify tables, create a primary key, and create a composite key.

Topic A: Planning and designing databases

This topic covers the following Microsoft Office Specialist exam objectives for Access 2013.

#	Objective
1.1	**Create a New Database**
1.1.1	Create new databases
1.1.2	Create databases use templates
1.5	**Print and Export a Database**
1.5.4	Save databases as templates

Planning databases

Explanation

Before you create a database, it's important to determine the type of data to be stored. For example, if you're keeping track of a company's products, sales, and retailers, you must plan and design a database that can store the related data. This data should be stored in three separate tables so you can distinguish between these three sets of information. You'll also need to plan how you'll be using the information stored in the database and what kind of reports you'll need to run. Thorough planning ensures that no data is missing or redundant, and it saves time on future modifications of the database.

To plan a database, you must determine:

- The purpose of the database
- The number of tables and the type of information you'll store in each table
- The fields that will be used in each table
- The types of queries you'll want to run against the database
- The forms you'll need to create
- The types of reports you'll need to generate

Stored vs. calculated data

When planning a database, you should determine which data should be stored and which data should be calculated. Stored data remains the same until a user changes it. Calculated data changes in response to other database updates.

For example, the price of an individual spice is typically a stored value; that is, it remains the same until a user changes it. But the total value of a spice held in inventory changes when the price does: if the price goes up, the value in inventory increases, and vice versa. The total inventory value, which depends on the price, is an example of data that should be calculated by the database rather than entered by the user.

Do it!

A-1: Planning a database

Questions and answers

1 You work in the Sales and Marketing department of Outlander Spices. You keep track of the company's retailers, and you want to create a database of information related to the operations in your department. What is the purpose of the database?

2 How many tables will you need to create, and what type of information do you need to store in each table?

3 Identify some of the fields that you'll need to create in the tables.

4 What kind of information could you extract from these tables by using queries?

5 If a database field tracks the quantity sold to a retailer, should that data be stored or calculated at runtime?

6 If a database field tracks the number of days outstanding for a retailer's invoice, should that data be stored or calculated at runtime?

Creating databases

Explanation

After you've planned and designed a database, you're ready to create it. You can create a database from a template or start with a blank database.

Rules for naming databases and objects

When naming a database or any database object, observe the following naming conventions:

- The name can contain letters, numbers, special characters, and embedded spaces.
- The name cannot start with a space.
- Database *file* names cannot contain more than 260 characters (for the entire path).
- Database *object* names cannot contain more than 64 characters.

It's good practice to use an underscore (_) instead of an embedded space in a database name or an object name. Object names cannot include a period (.), an exclamation mark (!), an accent grave (`), or brackets ([]).

Database templates

Access has database templates designed for various tasks. Some of these come with Access, and others can be downloaded from the Web. If you find a template that seems to fit your purpose, you can use it to create a database and then adjust it to suit your needs.

To create a database by using a template:

1 On the opening screen, select a template category.
2 Select the template that most closely describes what you need.
3 In the right pane, name the database and specify a location for it.
4 Click Create, or if the template is online, click Download.

Do it!

A-2:   Creating a database from a template

Files created for this activity are saved in Student Data folder **Unit 2\Topic A**.

Here's how	Here's why
1 On the opening screen, click **Desktop contacts**	 The Desktop contacts window appears.
2 Edit the File Name box to read **MyContacts**	
3 Beside the File Name box, click	To open the File New Database dialog box. You'll specify a location for the file.
Browse to the current topic folder	
Click **OK**	To close the dialog box. The location shown under the file name is now the current topic folder.
4 Click **Create**	To save and open the new database. The database opens, and a Getting Started window appears.
Click the Close button (X) in the upper-right corner of the Getting Started window.	(If necessary.) To close the window. The Contacts table displays.
5 Observe the fields in the table	This table has fields for entering contact information.

Saving user-defined templates

Explanation

You can save your own templates so that you can create a database from a structure you designed. You can save a template with or without data. User-created templates are available under Personal on the opening screen.

To save a database as a template, do this:

1 On the File tab, click Save As.

2 Under Save Database As, click Template and then click the Save As button. The Create New Template from This Database dialog box opens.

3 Enter a name, and fill out any other information you want. You can add icon and preview images.

4 If you check Application Part, the template will be available from the Create tab. If you check Include Data in Template, any data in the file will be saved with the template and will appear in the database you create using this template.

5 Click OK.

Do it!   **A-3:   Saving a user-defined template**

Here's how	Here's why
1 On the File tab, click **Save As**	The MyContacts database should still be open. You'll save this database as a template.
2 Under Save Database As, click **Template**	
Click **Save As**	The Create New Template from This Database dialog box opens.
3 In the Name box, enter **My Contacts Template**	
In the Description box, enter **Simple contact list**	
4 Check **Application Part**	So this template will appear under Application Parts on the ribbon.
5 Click **OK**	The Contact Management Database message box tells you that your template has been successfully saved.
Click **OK**	To close the message box.
6 Display the opening screen	On the File tab, click New.
Under the list of suggested searches, click **Personal**	My Contacts Template is available here. This is the template you just created.
On the File tab, click	The back button.
7 On the Create tab, click **Application Parts**	The template is also available under User Templates
8 Close the database	On the File tab, click Close.

Creating blank databases

Explanation

When you create a blank database, you'll initially see only the Database window. You must then manually create the objects to be included in the database. This manual method is more flexible because it results in custom tables and fields, instead of using a predefined design provided by a template.

To create a blank Access database:

1 Display the opening Access screen. (On the File tab, click New.)
2 Click Blank desktop database.
3 Specify the location and the name of the database.
4 Click Create.

Do it!

A-4: Creating a blank database

Here's how	Here's why
1 On the File tab, click **New** Click **Blank desktop database**	 Blank desktop database The Blank desktop database window appears.
2 Edit the File Name box to read **CreateDatabase**	
3 Beside the File Name box, click ▢	To open the File New Database dialog box. You'll specify a location for the file.
Browse to the current topic folder	
Click **OK**	To close the dialog box. The location shown under the file name is now the current topic folder.
4 Click **Create**	To save and open the new database. The database opens to an empty table in Datasheet view.
5 Close the database	

Topic B: Exploring tables

This topic covers the following Microsoft Office Specialist exam objectives for Access 2013.

#	Objective
1.3	**Navigate through a Database**
1.3.5	Change views

Explanation

Access provides four views for working with tables. The views are Datasheet, Design, PivotTable, and PivotChart.

Views

Datasheet view displays data in a tabular format, with rows and columns. Use Datasheet view to scroll through records and to add, edit, or view data in a table.

If you want to change the design of a table by adding or changing field details, you can do it in Design view. Design view gives you complete control over the table's structure.

To switch between Datasheet view and Design view, use the View buttons in the status bar or the View button on the ribbon.

Use PivotTable view to analyze data. Use PivotChart view to display data graphically.

Contextual tabs

The ribbon changes, and different tabs appear, depending on what kind of database object you are working with and which view is active. When you open a table in Datasheet view, two "Table Tools" tabs appear on the ribbon: Fields and Table. When you open a table in Design view, the Table Tools | Design tab appears on the ribbon.

Do it!

B-1: Discussing views

Questions and answers

1 When you want to add or edit data in a table, which view will you work with?

2 If you want to change the structure of a table, which view will you use?

3 Which view will help you in analyzing data?

4 You want to present the analysis of sales data in a meeting. Which view will you use?

Datasheet view

Explanation
By default, tables open in Datasheet view, shown in Exhibit 2-1. Each column is a field, and each row is a record. Use the navigation buttons and scrollbars to scroll through the table. You can scroll to the left or the right by using the horizontal scrollbar. You can scroll up and down by using the vertical scrollbar.

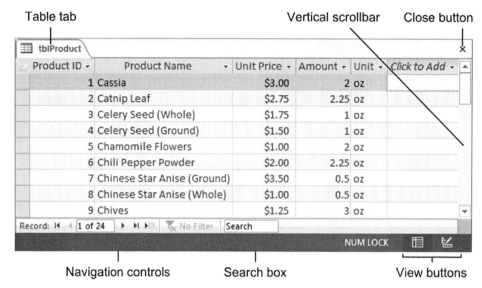

Exhibit 2-1: The tblProduct table in Datasheet view

Do it!
B-2: Examining a table in Datasheet view

The files for this activity are in Student Data folder **Unit 2\Topic B**.

Here's how	Here's why
1 Open Retailers	Click the File tab and click Open.
2 In the Navigation Pane, double-click **tblProduct**	To open the tblProduct window, shown in Exhibit 2-1. The tblProduct table is shown in Datasheet view. The Fields and Table tabs appear on the ribbon, under Table Tools.
3 Observe the fields in the table	Each column in the table represents a field. The fields are Product ID, Product Name, Unit Price, Amount, and Unit. You can add a new field by adding data under "Click to Add."
Observe the records in the table	Each row in the table represents a record. There are 24 records in the table. You can add, edit, or delete records in Datasheet view.
Observe the lower-left area of the Datasheet window	In this area, "1 of 24" appears, indicating that the first record is now active and that there are 24 records in the table.

Navigating in a table

Explanation   In Datasheet view, you can navigate in a table by using the navigation buttons, shown in Exhibit 2-2. These are located at the bottom of the Datasheet view window.

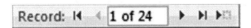

Exhibit 2-2: The navigation buttons and the record number box in Datasheet view

The following table describes the navigation buttons and the record number box.

Item	Description
⏮	First record in the table
◀	Previous record
1 of 24	Current active record in the table
▶	Next record
⏭	Last record
▶※	New (blank) record

Using the record selector

You can also navigate through records and select specific records by using the *record selector*, which points to the active record and indicates its status. The record selector is the small box to the left of each record in a table. If you click in this box, the record next to it is highlighted, making it the active record.

	Product ID ▾	Product Name ▾	Unit Price ▾	Amount ▾	Unit ▾	Click to Add ▾
	1	Cassia	$3.00	2	oz	
	2	Catnip Leaf	$2.75	2.25	oz	
	3	Celery Seed (Whole)	$1.75	1	oz	
	4	Celery Seed (Ground)	$1.50	1	oz	
	5	Chamomile Flowers	$1.00	2	oz	

tblProduct

Exhibit 2-3: A table with a selected record

The icon for the record selector changes based on the status of the record. When you click a specific field in a record, both the record selector and the field name are highlighted in orange. The following table explains the icons for the record selector:

Icon	Description
	Indicates that you are in the process of editing the record but have not yet saved it.
	Indicates that you can enter data for a new record.

Do it!

B-3: Navigating a table in Datasheet view

Here's how	Here's why
1 Verify that the tblProduct table is open in Datasheet view	
	The record selector is highlighted to the left of the data value 1.
2 Observe the record number box	1 of 24
	(At the bottom of the Datasheet view window.) It indicates that record 1 is the active record.
Click ▶	(The Next record button is at the bottom of the Datasheet window.) To move to the next record. The record selector moves to the left side of 2.
Observe the record number box	The record number box now reads 2 of 24.
3 Click ◀	To move to the previous record. The record selector is positioned to the left of the first row.
4 Click ▶|	To move to the last record. The record selector is now next to the twenty-fourth record. Note that the record number is not the same as the product ID number.
5 Click |◀	To move to the first record.
Edit the record number box to read **5**	You'll move to the fifth record.
Press ↵ ENTER	The record selector is next to the fifth record.

6 Click ▶*	To add a new record.
7 In the Product Name field of the new record, enter **Ancho Pepper (Ground)**	The value in the Product ID field automatically changes to 35. This occurs because the Product ID field is set to a numeric data type that will automatically increment by one each time you add a record.
Observe the record selector	It shows a pencil, indicating that you are in the process of editing a record.
Press (TAB)	To move to the next cell.
8 In the Unit Price field, enter **12.75**	Access inserts the $ automatically because this field is formatted to display values as currency.
Press (TAB)	To move to the next cell.
In the Amount field, enter **2**	
In the Unit field, enter **oz**	
9 Press (TAB) twice	To move to the next record. Changes in a record are saved automatically when you move to a different record or close the table.

Design view

Explanation

The design of a table includes field names, the type of data stored in each field, the field size, and the manner in which field values appear in the table. When you want to specify the properties of a field, such as Field Name and Data Type, you use Design view. In this view, the window is split into top and bottom panes, as shown in Exhibit 2-4.

If the table you want to design is already open, you can switch to Design view by clicking the Design View button in the window's status bar or by clicking View on the ribbon and choosing Table Design. You can also right-click the object's tab and choose Design View from the shortcut menu.

If the table you want to change is not open, you can open it directly into Design view by right-clicking the table's name in the Navigation Pane and choosing Design View.

The upper pane displays the design of the table in the following terms:

- **Field Name** — The name of each field.
- **Data Type** — The type of data stored in each field. For example, the Text data type stores text values, and Number data type stores numbers.
- **Description** — An explanation of the field's purpose.

The lower pane is the Field Properties pane. Here, you can see the properties, or attributes, of each field, including Field Size, Format, and Caption. The Format property specifies the way the data should appear in the table. The Caption property is used to specify titles for fields. These captions appear as field headings in the Datasheet view of the table. If you don't specify captions for the fields, the field names appear as the field headings. The other field properties vary depending on the field's data type.

Exhibit 2-4: The tblProduct table in Design view

Do it!   **B-4: Examining a table in Design view**

Here's how	Here's why
1 Click ▤	(The Design View button is in the window's status bar.) To switch to Design view.
2 Observe the window	The tblProduct window appears in Design view, as shown in Exhibit 2-4. The Table Tools | Design tab appears on the ribbon.
3 Observe the Field Name column	The Field Name column lists the fields in the table: lngProductID, strProductName, curUnitPrice, lngAmount, and strUnit. The corresponding field headings in Datasheet view are Product ID, Product Name, Unit Price, Amount, and Unit.
4 Observe the Data Type column	The data type for lngProductID is AutoNumber; the data type for strProductName and strUnit is Text; the data type for lngAmount is Number; and the data type for curUnitPrice is Currency.
5 Observe the Description column	Each field has a description.
6 Observe the Field Properties pane	This pane shows the field properties specific to different data types. Exhibit 2-4 shows the properties of the lngProductID field.
7 Close the table window	Click the Close button in the upper-right corner of the table window.
8 Close the database	Click the File tab and click Close.

Topic C: Creating tables

This topic covers the following Microsoft Office Specialist exam objectives for Access 2013.

#	Objective
1.2	**Manage Relationships and Keys**
1.2.3	Set primary key fields
2.1	**Create a Table**
2.1.1	Create new tables
2.1.5	Create tables from templates and application parts
2.2	**Format a Table**
2.2.4	Add table descriptions
2.2.5	Rename tables
2.3	**Manage Records**
2.3.2	Add new records
2.4	**Create and Modify Fields**
2.4.1	Add fields to tables
2.4.5	Change field data types
2.4.6	Configure fields to auto-increment

Methods of creating tables

Explanation

Tables are the heart of the database. This is where the data is stored. Most other objects—forms, queries, and reports—are based on he data found in tables.

After creating a database, you need to create tables in which to store the data. By default, Access creates one new blank table when you create a database. You can create additional tables in any of the following ways:

- By using the table templates
- By using Design view
- By using Datasheet view
- By copying the structure of an existing table

After creating a table, you can add fields to it and set the primary key. A *primary key* is a field that uniquely identifies each record in a table. For example, you can use a separate number for each retailer; these numbers will uniquely identify the retailers. After you've created a table from a table template, you can modify field names, data types, field sizes, or other field properties in Design view.

When you create a table in Datasheet view, the table opens with nondescript field names and no set data types. Although this approach might be acceptable for some quick tasks, you will probably want to start with a template or a custom-designed table in Design view.

Using the Quick Start table templates

Like the database templates, Quick Start table templates provide you with a starting point, a rough draft that you can then modify to suit your needs. To create a table:

1 Open the database in which you want to create a table.

2 Click the Create tab.

3 To start with a table template, click Application Parts on the ribbon and select a template under Quick Start. To start with a blank table, click Table in the Tables group.

4 To add a column, click the "Click to Add" heading and select a data type. Then rename the new column. (You can also add fields by using the Data Type gallery, discussed later in this topic.)

5 To rename a column, right-click the field name and choose Rename Field. Enter a new name.

6 To delete a column, right-click the field name and choose Delete Field.

7 To modify the table in more detail, switch to Design view.

8 To rename the table, close it. Then right-click the table name, choose Rename, and enter a new name.

Do it!

C-1:   Creating a table from a table template

The files for this activity are in Student Data folder **Unit 2\Topic C**.

Here's how	Here's why
1 Open Projects	It's a blank database.
2 Click the **Create** tab	On the ribbon.
3 In the Templates group, click **Application Parts** and select **Tasks**	(In the Quick Start group.) The Tasks table and two forms appear in the Navigation Pane.
4 In the Navigation Pane, double-click **Tasks**	The table opens in Datasheet view.
5 Right-click the field name **Task Title** and choose **Rename Field**	You'll rename this field and add columns to make this table suit your needs.
Edit the field name to read **Project**	
6 Click **Click to Add** and choose **Short Text**	(At the top of the last field.) A new column named Field1 appears, with the name selected for editing.
Rename the new field **Assigned to**	It's already selected; just enter the new name.

7	Switch to Design view	Click the Design View button on the ribbon.
	Observe the fields and data types	The ID field is a unique identifier and is set as the primary key.
8	Close the table	Right-click the table tab and choose Close, or click the X in the upper-right corner of the table window.
9	In the Navigation Pane, right-click the table name and choose **Rename**	You'll give this table a more meaningful name.
	Edit the name to read **Projects** and press (↵ ENTER)	
10	Right-click the table name and choose **Table Properties**	The tblProjects Properties dialog box opens. You'll add a table description.
	Edit the Description box to read **Project tasking and assignments**	
	Click **OK**	To save the table description and close the tblProjects Properties dialog box.
11	Close the database	

Creating tables in Design view

Explanation
To create a table in Design view:

1 Open the database in which you want to create the table.
2 Click the Create tab.
3 Click the Table Design button in the Tables group.

You can also create a table—with or without a template—in Datasheet view and then switch to Design view.

You can then enter the necessary information, such as adding field names and descriptions in the Field Name and Description columns. Another column, Data Type, contains a drop-down arrow that you can use to select a data type from the list.

Design view contains a row selector, which indicates the active field with a black triangle, as shown in Exhibit 2-5. The lower pane is the Field Properties pane, which contains two tabs: General and Lookup. Use the General tab to set field properties, such as the size of a field. Use the Lookup tab to modify field properties, such as the appearance of a field in a table.

Exhibit 2-5: A new table in Design view

Do it!

C-2:   Creating a table in Design view

Here's how	Here's why
1 Open Sales	You'll use Design view to create a table in this database.
2 Click the **Create** tab	
3 Click **Table Design**	(In the Tables group.) To open a new table in Design view.
4 Observe the table title	The title is Table1.
Observe the upper pane of the window	The highlighted row selector is positioned to the left of the first record.
Observe the Field Properties pane	This pane has two tabs: General and Lookup. By default, the General tab is active.

Adding fields

Explanation

You can use various data types, such as text or number, depending on the type of data the field should store. For example, if you want to store addresses or product codes that contain characters, numbers, or a combination of both, choose the Text data type.

To add a text field:

1 In Design view, place the insertion point in the Field Name column, and enter a name for the field.

2 Press Tab to move to the Data Type column. Click the drop-down arrow and select Text from the Data Type list.

3 Press Tab to move to the Description column. Enter a description of the field.

The following table describes some of the data types, along with the size and type of data they can store:

Data type	Size	Type of data stored
Short Text	Up to 255 characters.	Text or a combination of text and numbers, such as an address, name, or phone number.
Long Text	Up to 64,000 characters.	Long text, such as comments or notes.
Number	Several sizes available to store numbers with varying degrees of precision.	Numeric information used in calculations.
Date/Time	Accommodates dates and time across thousands of years.	Dates and times, such as 10/23/2013 2:00:00 PM.
Currency	Up to 15 digits to the left of the decimal point and 4 digits to the right.	Monetary values, such as $5.00.
AutoNumber	N/A	A number that increments automatically with each new record. It can be used to provide a unique ID for a record, and it's often used for primary keys.
Yes/No	Size controlled by Access.	One of two values: Yes or No.
OLE object	Up to 2 GB of data.	Images, documents, graphs, and other objects.
Hyperlink	Up to 1 GB of data.	Internet or LAN addresses.
Attachment		Images, workbook files, documents, and other types of files. Unlike OLE objects, attached files can be viewed and edited, and require less storage space.
Calculated	Conforms to the size of the result data type.	The result of an expression or formula that you can create.
Lookup	N/A	Links to lists in other tables, or a list of user-defined values. Also called a *multi-value field*.

The Number data type provides field size settings. Field sizes that can accommodate large or complex numbers use more storage space than do field sizes for smaller numbers. You should choose field sizes that are appropriate for the type of numeric data to be stored. If the field size is too small, the data cannot be stored. If it is too large, the database will grow unnecessarily large.

Field size	Description	Decimals	Size (in bytes)
Byte	Whole numbers from 0 to 255	None	1
Integer	Whole numbers from –32,68 to 32,767	None	2
Long Integer	(The default.) Whole numbers from -2,147,483,648 to 2,147,483,647	None	4
Single	Decimal values from -3.4×10^{38} to 3.4×10^{38}	0-7	4
Double	Decimal values from -1.797×10^{308} to 1.797×10^{308}	0-15	8
Replication ID	A *Globally Unique Identifier (GUID)* used to identify database objects when replicating databases	N/A	16
Decimal	Decimal values from -10^{28} to 10^{28}	0-28	12

The default size for a Short Text field is 50 characters. However, you can change the field size by using the General tab in the Field Properties pane. You can't assign the Text data type to a field if you want to enter a date in it or perform calculations. For dates or numerals, you assign data types such as Date/Time or Number.

The Long Text data type stores longer strings of characters and numbers than will fit in a Short Text field. For example, a Long Text field could be used to store a set of notes on a specific sale.

To add fields of any data type to your table, enter the field name in the Field Name column and select the data type from the Data Type list.

Boolean operations

When choosing a data type for a field, consider the way the field will be used in database operations. If the field will need to support searches or comparisons, be sure to use a data type that supports Boolean operators such as `and`, `or`, `not`, and comparison operators such as `equal`, `not equal`, and `less than`. The data types that lend themselves most easily to Boolean operations include:

- Short Text
- Number
- Date/Time
- Currency
- Yes/No
- AutoNumber

C-3: Adding fields and descriptions to a table

Here's how	Here's why
1 In the Field Name column, enter **lngSaleID**	To name the first field in the table.
Press (TAB)	To move to the Data Type column. You'll see a drop-down arrow.
2 Click the drop-down arrow	Short Text ▾ Short Text Long Text Number Date/Time Currency AutoNumber Yes/No OLE Object Hyperlink Attachment Calculated Lookup Wizard...
	To display the Data Type list. By default, Short Text is selected. You'll change the data type for this field.
From the Data Type list, select **AutoNumber**	This will be the data type for the lngSaleID field. Each time a record is added to the table, this field will increment automatically.
Press (TAB)	To move to the Description column.
In the Description column, enter **Unique sale identifier**	
3 Press (TAB)	The row selector moves to the next field row.
In the Field Name column, enter **strProductID**	To name the second field.
Press (TAB)	To move to the Data Type column. Short Text is selected as the data type.
4 Press (TAB)	To accept Short Text as the data type and move to the Description column. If the Product ID field will be used in searches or comparisons, then making this a Short Text field will help to ensure that Boolean operations execute efficiently.
In the Description column, enter **Product code**	

5 Press ⟨TAB⟩	The row selector moves to the next field row.
Enter **strSalesperson**	To name the third field.
Press ⟨TAB⟩	To move to the Data Type column. Short Text is selected as the data type.
6 In the Field Name column, click in the fourth row	You'll skip the descriptions and add another field to the table.
Enter **lngQuantitySold**	To name the fourth field.
Press ⟨TAB⟩	You'll select a data type for the lngQuantitySold field.
From the Data Type list, select **Number**	This field will store the number of units (pounds or kg) sold, rather than the sales amount in dollars. A number field is required rather than a currency field.
7 In the Field Properties pane at the bottom of the window, click beside **Long Integer**	

General	Lookup
Field Size	Long Integer ▾
Format	Byte
Decimal Places	Integer
Input Mask	Long Integer
Caption	Single
Default Value	Double
Validation Rule	Replication ID
Validation Text	Decimal

	The list of Field Sizes appears.
Observe the Field Sizes	You'll keep Long Integer as the field size because decimal values are not required, and a large customer might conceivably order more than 32,767 units of an item.
8 Add the field **curSaleAmount**	This field will store the amount of the sale.
From the Data Type list, select **Currency**	This will be the data type for the curSaleAmount field.
9 Add the field **dtmDateOfSale**	This field will store the date on which a sale was made.
From the Data Type list, select **Date/Time**	This will be the data type for the dtmDateOfSale field.
10 Add the field **ysnDiscount**	This field will store the status of the availability of discounts for specific products.
From the Data Type list, select **Yes/No**	This will be the data type for the Discount field.
In the Description field, enter **Does this sale qualify for a discount?**	

11	Add the field **ltxNotes**	This will be the sixth field. It will store details about sales.
	From the Data Type list, select **Long Text**	Notes about a sale might require more than the 255 characters available in a short text field.
	In the Description column, enter **Notes about a specific sale**	

Setting the primary key for a table

Explanation

Sometimes you might find that two records in a table have the same value, making it difficult to differentiate between them. For example, a field called strSalesperson could store duplicate values if two or more salespeople have the same name. That would make this field a poor choice for the primary key, which should be a unique identifier for each record in the database. A better choice might be an AutoNumber ID field.

To set a field as a primary key, do either of the following:

- Select the field and click Primary Key on the Design tab.
- Right-click the field row and choose Primary Key from the shortcut menu.

Do it!

C-4: Setting the primary key

Here's how	Here's why
1 In the Field Name column, place the insertion point in the third row	You'll set the strSalesperson field as the primary key.
2 On the Design tab, click **Primary Key**	
	A key icon appears to the left of strSalesperson to show that it is now the primary key. However, the strSalesperson field is not a good choice for primary key because the values in this field can repeat within the database.
3 In the Field Name column, place the insertion point in the first row	You'll set lngSaleID, the default AutoNumber field, as the primary key instead.
4 Click **Primary Key**	A key icon appears to the left of lngSaleID to show that it is now the primary key. At this point, the view should resemble Exhibit 2-5.

Saving tables

Explanation

After you have completed the table design, you need to save it. You can save a table by right-clicking the table tab and choosing Save. This launches the Save As dialog box, as shown in Exhibit 2-6. You need to provide a name for the table before saving it for the first time. You can also save a table by clicking the File tab and choosing Save As, Save Object As, Save As.

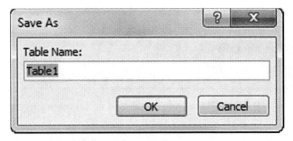

Exhibit 2-6: The Save As dialog box

Do it!

C-5:   Saving the table

Here's how	Here's why
1 Right-click the table tab	
Click **Save**	To open the Save As dialog box, shown in Exhibit 2-6.
2 Edit the Table Name box to read **tblSales**	You'll save the table as tblSales.
Click **OK**	To save the table.
3 Click the **Home** tab	The table name is now shown in the Navigation Pane.

Adding records

Explanation
After you create and save a table, you can enter data in it. To do so, you need to open the table in Datasheet view. After you type data into a record, Access automatically saves it when you move the insertion point out of that record.

Here are two ways to enter data in a table:

- Click the New record navigation button, and enter your data.
- Place the insertion point in a field in the first blank row, and enter your data.

Do it!

C-6: Adding a record

Here's how	Here's why
1 Switch to Datasheet view	You'll add a record to the table.
2 In the strProductID column, enter **101**	strProductID ▾ 101
	This is the product ID for the first product.
Observe the lngSaleID field	When you entered data in this record, the lngSaleID field automatically inserted a 1 because this is an AutoNumber field.
3 Press (TAB)	To move to the next field.
4 In the strSalesperson column, enter **Bill MacArthur**	strSalespers ▾ Bill MacArthur
	This is the salesperson's name for the first record.
5 Point to the l'ne between the second and third field names	You'll resize the columns to see the whole field name.
Drag the border as indicated	）ers ▾ sng╬uant Arthur
6 Resize the other columns as necessary	So you can see the whole field names.
7 Edit the lngQuantitySold column to read **30**	

8 Edit the curSaleAmount column to read **625.5**

The format changes when you leave the field. The default format is Auto, which displays a dollar sign and two decimal places.

9 In the dtmDateOfSale column, enter **6/19/13**

When you leave the field, the format changes to show a four-digit year. The default format is mm/dd/yyyy.

10 In the ysnDiscount column, check as shown

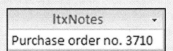

There are only two possible values for a yes/no field. This kind of field is also called a true/false or Boolean field.

11 In the ltxNotes column, enter **Purchase order no. 3710**

ltxNotes ▾
Purchase order no. 3710

Resize the column to see all of this.

12 Right-click the table tab and choose **Close**

A message box prompts you to save changes.

Click **Yes**

To close the table and save the layout changes. The data itself is saved as you leave each field.

Copying and modifying tables

Explanation

You can create a new table by copying the structure of an existing table. To copy a table:

1 In the Navigation Pane, right-click the table to be copied and choose Copy.

2 Right-click any blank area in the Navigation Pane and choose Paste to open the Paste Table As dialog box, shown in Exhibit 2-7.

3 Edit the Table Name box to give the table a new name.

4 Under Paste Options, select Structure Only.

5 Click OK.

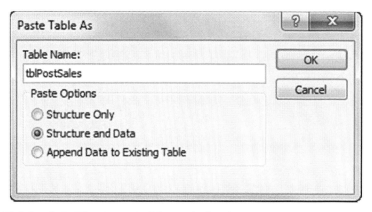

Exhibit 2-7: The Paste Table As dialog box

Renaming and deleting tables

When you right-click a table in the Navigation Pane, a shortcut menu appears. You can use it for many operations, including renaming and deleting tables.

Do it!

C-7: Copying, modifying, and deleting a table

Here's how	Here's why
1 In the Navigation Pane, right-click **tblSales**	The shortcut menu appears. You'll create a table by copying this table's structure.
Choose **Copy**	To copy tblSales. The shortcut menu closes.
2 Point to a blank area of the Navigation Pane and right-click	The shortcut menu appears.
Choose **Paste**	The Paste Table As dialog box appears.
3 Edit the Table Name box to read **tblPostSales**	To name the new table.
4 Under Paste Options, select **Structure Only**	To copy only the table structure to the new table.
Click **OK**	To close the dialog box and create the table. The new table appears in the Navigation Pane.
5 Open tblPostSales in Design view	Right-click the table and choose Design View.
Observe the fields	The structure of this table is identical to tblSales.
6 Switch to Datasheet view	(Right-click the table tab and choose Datasheet View.) The table is empty of data because only the structure was copied.
Close tblPostSales	
7 Right-click **tblPostSales** and choose **Rename**	The table name becomes editable.
Edit the table name to read **discard**	
8 Right-click the table and choose **Delete**	You'll remove this table from the database. The Microsoft Office Access dialog box appears.
Click **Yes**	To confirm that you want to delete the table. The table is removed from the Navigation Pane.
Close the database	

Setting two primary keys for a table

Explanation

You can define two fields as the primary key for a table. This type of primary key is called a *composite key*. It is also called a *compound key* or a *multi-field key*.

Composite keys are typically used if a table has no single field (with a set of unique values) that can serve as the primary key. However, there may be two or more fields which, when combined, create a unique value. These fields can be defined as the composite key.

To define two or more fields as a composite key:

1 Open the table in Design view.
2 Press and hold Ctrl.
3 Select the first row that will be part of the composite key.
4 Select the next row or rows that will be part of the composite key.
5 Release the Ctrl key.
6 On the ribbon, click Primary Key.

A key icon appears beside each row that is part of the composite key, as shown in Exhibit 2-8.

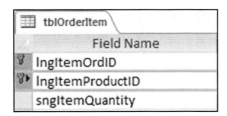

Exhibit 2-8: A table with a composite key

Do it! ### C-8: Creating a composite key

The files for this activity are in Student Data folder **Unit 2\Topic C**.

Here's how	Here's why
1 Open Reports	From the current topic folder.
2 Open **tblOrderItem**	You'll create a composite key for this table.
Observe the Order ID field	There are multiple occurrences of each Order ID. This field cannot be used as the primary key because the values are not unique.
Observe the Product field	This field also has repeated values and cannot be used as the primary key. However, each combination of Order ID and Product provides a unique value.
3 Switch to Design view	Right-click the table tab and choose Design View.
Observe the fields in the database	There is no key icon in the far left column. This table has no primary key.
4 Select the first row	(If necessary.) Click the column to the left of lngItemOrdID.
Press and hold ⌨CTRL	
Select the second row	Click the column to the left of lngItemProductID.
Release ⌨CTRL	
5 Click **Primary Key**	(On the Design tab.) To make both fields the primary key.
6 Observe the table	A key icon appears in the column beside each row. Both fields constitute the primary key, as shown in Exhibit 2-8.
7 Close the table	(Right-click the table tab and choose Close.) The Microsoft Office Access dialog box appears, prompting you to save changes.
Click **Yes**	To save the changes.
8 Close the database	

The Data Type gallery

Explanation

The Data Type gallery gives you a longer list of data types than that provided in the Data Type list you see when you add a field from the data sheet. The gallery also provides Quick Start fields, which are sets of fields for common data types, such as name and address, that you can add and then modify. To use the Data Type gallery, select the new column and click the More Fields button in the Add & Delete group on the Table Tools | Fields tab.

Do it!

C-9: Using the Data Type gallery

The files for this activity are in Student Data folder **Unit 2\Topic C**.

Here's how	Here's why
1 Open Contacts	From the current topic folder.
2 Click the **Create** tab	You'll make a new table and use the Data Type gallery to add fields.
3 In the Tables group, click **Table**	A new, blank table appears in Datasheet view, and the Fields and Table tabs appear on the ribbon.
4 On the Fields tab, click **More Fields**	(In the Add & Delete group.) To open the Data Type gallery.
5 Scroll down the Quick Start section and click **Name**	
6 Delete the **First Name** field	Right-click the column heading and choose Delete Field.
7 Click in the first field under "Click to Add"	(Don't click the heading.) You'll add another set of Quick Start Fields.
8 Under Quick Start in the Data Type gallery, click **Address**	Several address-related fields are added.
9 Save the table as **tblContacts**	
10 Close the database	

Unit summary: Databases and tables

Topic A   In this topic, you learned how to **plan a database**. You learned about the importance of following the **naming rules** while creating a database and its objects. You also learned how to create a blank database and how to **create a database** by using the database templates. Finally, you learned that you have more flexibility when creating a blank database.

Topic B   In this topic, you learned how to use various views, such as **Design** and **Datasheet** views. You learned that you can use Datasheet view to scroll through records, and use Design view to change a table's design. You also learned how to examine a table in Datasheet view and in Design view.

Topic C   In this topic, you learned how to **create a table** by using the table templates and how to modify a table in Design view. In addition, you learned how to create a table in Design view. You also learned how to **add fields** to a table, set the **primary key**, and save a table. Next, you learned how to add records to a table. Then, you learned how to create a table by **copying the structure** of another table. You learned how to rename and delete tables, and how to define a **composite key** for a table. Finally, you learned how to add sets of fields to a table by using the Data Type gallery.

Review questions

1 Why would you use database templates to create a database?

2 What is the advantage of creating a database manually?

3 Which of the following views displays data in a tabular format with rows and columns?

   A Design view

   B Datasheet view

   C Chart view

   D PivotTable view

4 Which view is used to add field details?

5 In Datasheet view, how do you move between records?

6 Which view is used to enter data in a table?

Independent practice activity

In this activity, you'll plan and create a database. You'll use a template to create a table for this database. Next, you'll add records and set the primary key. Finally, you'll add data and save the table and database.

1 Plan and design a database for storing information about customers who place orders for different products. The database should have a minimum of two tables.

2 Create a new blank database with a name of your choice. Save it in the current Unit summary folder.

3 Close the default table. Delete it if necessary. (*Hint:* Right-click the table name and choose Delete.)

4 Create a table by using the Quick Start template of your choice. (*Hint:* Click the Create tab to start.)

5 Change and add fields to suit your intended purpose. Use Quick Start fields, if appropriate.

6 Save and close the table.

7 Create a table in Design view. Add the fields and set the primary key shown in Exhibit 2-9.

8 Save the table as **tblCustomerOrder**.

9 Enter data in tblCustomerOrder as shown in Exhibit 2-10. Adjust column widths as necessary.

10 Save and close the table.

11 Close the database.

	Field Name	Data Type	Description (Optional)
🔑	lngOrderNo	AutoNumber	Order number, automatically generated by Access
	strProductID	Short Text	Product ID number
	dtmOrderDate	Date/Time	Date the order was placed
	strCustomer	Short Text	Name of customer who placed the order
	lngOrderQuantity	Number	Quantity of product ordered
	ysnDispatched	Yes/No	Has the order already been dispatched?

Exhibit 2-9: The tblCustomerOrder table in Design view after Step 7

lngOrderNo ⏷	strProductID ⏷	dtmOrderDate ⏷	strCustomer ⏷	lngOrderQuantity ⏷	ysnDispatch ⏷
1	1	6/19/2013	Rebecca Austin	250	☑
2	2	7/11/2013	Annie Phillips	367	☐
3	3	7/15/2013	Julie Stone	234	☐

Exhibit 2-10: The records in the tblCustomerOrder table after Step 9

Unit 3
Fields and records

Complete this unit, and you'll know how to:

A Modify a table design by changing field names, inserting and deleting fields, moving fields, and using the Attachment data type.

B Find and replace data in a table, and hide and freeze fields.

C Sort, filter, and delete records.

Topic A: Changing the design of a table

This topic covers the following Microsoft Office Specialist exam objectives for Access 2013.

#	Objective
2.2	**Format a Table**
2.2.3	Add total rows
2.4	**Create and Modify Fields**
2.4.1	Add fields to tables
2.4.3	Change field captions
2.4.9	Delete fields

Modifying fields

Explanation

After you create a table, you can edit its design. You can delete fields, insert new fields, change field names, or change the order in which fields appear. You make these changes in Design view.

Effective field names

It will be easier for you and others to use your database if you give each field a name that reflects its purpose. For example, the field name ProductName is easier to understand than the field name Pname. Exhibit 3-1 shows a table with field names that are not very meaningful.

	Field Name	Data Type	Description (Optional)
🔑	PrID	AutoNumber	Unique ID automatically assigned to each new product
	Pname	Short Text	Full name of product as it appears in catalog
	Up	Currency	Price of each unit of product
	Amount	Number	Amount of each unit of product
	strUnit	Short Text	Unit of measurement
	Disco	Yes/No	Discount available?

Exhibit 3-1: A table with uninformative field names

Ideally, the name of a field should be self-explanatory. To make the field names clear and readable, use a combination of uppercase and lowercase letters. It's also helpful if you use consistent naming conventions and names that reflect both the field's data type and its purpose. It is a common convention to begin a field name with a lowercase abbreviation of the data type, followed by capitalized descriptive words.

The following table shows some examples of field names:

Data type	Purpose	Field name
Short text	Employee last name	strEmpLastName
Long text	Product description	ltxItemDesc
Number (long integer)	Employee number	lngEmpID
Number (single byte)	Inventory amount	sngAmount
Date	Shipping date	dtmShipDate
Currency	Product cost	curProductCost
Hyperlink	Supplier Web site	hypSupplierHome

You can change any field name in Design view by selecting the name and editing it. Changing the field name does not affect the data already in the table.

Do it!

A-1:   Modifying field names

The files for this activity are in Student Data folder **Unit 3\Topic A**.

Here's how	Here's why
1 Open Employees1	
2 In the Navigation Pane, right-click **tblProduct** and choose **Design View**	To open the table in Design view. You'll analyze the design of this table.
3 Under the Field Name column, observe the field names PrID and Pname	You'll change the field names to make them more self-explanatory.
4 Select **PrID**	If necessary.
Enter **lngProductID**	This will be the new name for the first field ("lng" stands for "long integer").
5 Change the other field names as shown	Field Name: lngProductID / strProductName / curUnitPrice / sngAmount / strUnit / ysnDiscount
6 Right-click the table tab and click **Save**	To update the table.

Deleting and inserting fields in a table

Explanation

After you create a table, you might find that you need to add or delete fields. You must select a field before you can delete it or insert a field above it.

Selecting a field

You can select a field by clicking its row selector, shown in Exhibit 3-2. When you move the pointer over the row selector, it changes to an arrow. Clicking the row selector highlights the row with a thick border. You can now delete this field or insert a new field above it.

tblProduct		
Field Name	Data Type	Description (Optional)
lngProductID	AutoNumber	Unique ID automatically assigned to each new product
strProductName	Short Text	Full name of product as it appears in catalog
curUnitPrice	Currency	Price of each unit of product
sngAmount	Number	Amount of each unit of product
strUnit	Short Text	Unit of measurement
ysnDiscount	Yes/No	Discount available?

Exhibit 3-2: A table with the last field selected

Deleting a field

To delete a field in Design view, select the field and then either press the Delete key or click Delete Rows on the Table Tools | Design tab. For example, in the tblProduct table, if you want to delete the ysnDiscount field, first select the field, as shown in Exhibit 3-2, and then press Delete. Access prompts you to confirm the deletion if the field contains data or if the field is a primary key. Access will not prompt you if the field is empty.

Inserting a field

In Design view, you can insert a field either at the end of the table or above an existing field. To insert a field above an existing field, select the field above which you want to insert the new field, and click Insert Rows. To add a new field at the end, just enter a field name in the first empty row.

Captions

By default, the field name appears at the top of its column in Datasheet view. But field names, while they contain useful information for the developer, are not always helpful for end-users. Therefore, for the benefit of the end-user, you can enter a caption for a field. The caption appears in place of the field name in all views except for Design view. To enter a caption in Design view, select a field and enter its caption on the General tab in the Field Properties pane.

Do it!   ## A-2:   Deleting and inserting fields

Here's how	Here's why
1 Click the row selector for the ysnDiscount field, as shown	→ | ysnDiscount Yes/No
	To select the field. The pointer changes into a black arrow when it's over a row selector.
2 In the Tools group, click ✕ Delete Rows	(On the Design tab.) A message box asks if you want to permanently delete the selected field and all of its data.
Click **Yes**	To delete the ysnDiscount field from the table.
3 Select the **curUnitPrice** row	You'll insert a field above this field.
4 Click ⅔= Insert Rows	A blank row appears above the row for the curUnitPrice field. The insertion point is in the first cell of the new row.
Under Field Name, in the inserted row, enter **sngMinQuantity**	To specify the new field name. This field stores data for the minimum quantity to be stored for each product.
Under Data Type, select **Number**	
Under Description, enter **Minimum quantity stored**	
5 In the Field Size property box, select **Single**	To make this a single-byte numeric value.
6 In the Caption property box, enter **Minimum**	General | Lookup |
	Field Size — Single
	Format
	Decimal Places — Auto
	Input Mask
	Caption — Minimum
	Default Value
	On the General tab in the Field Properties pane.
7 On the Quick Access toolbar, click 🖫	(The Save button.) To update the table. You should update tables whenever you modify them.

Moving fields

Explanation

If you enter the field details in an unsuitable sequence when you create a table, you might want to rearrange the fields by moving the field rows in Design view.

To move a field row:

1 Select the field row by using the row selector.

2 Drag the row selector to its new place in the list. The pointer changes to an arrow with a box. When you drop the field, the field row in that position automatically shifts down to the next row.

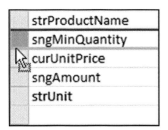

Exhibit 3-3: The pointer when you're moving a field

Do it!

A-3: Moving a field

Here's how	Here's why
1 Select the row for the field sngMinQuantity	(Click the row selector for the field.) You'll move this field below the field strUnit.
2 Drag the sngMinQuantity row selector to the row below strUnit	(As shown in Exhibit 3-3.) The mouse pointer changes to an arrow with a box, indicating that you can drag the field to a new location. When you see a heavy black line below strUnit, you'll know you're moving the row to the correct position. The entire row for sngMinQuantity is mo ed here.
3 Update the table	Click the Save button, or right-click the table tab and choose Save.

The Attachment data type

Explanation

The Attachment data type can be used to provide more detail about table data. You can use it to include documents, graphics, or other files as attachments to a field.

To use the Attachment data type:

1 Open a table in Design view.

2 Add a field to house the attachment for a record.

3 Under Data Type, select Attachment.

4 Save the table.

5 Switch to Datasheet view.

6 Right-click the Attachment field for the first record and choose Manage Attachments to open the Attachments dialog box.

7 Click Add to open the Choose File dialog box.

8 Select the desired file(s) and click Open.

9 Click OK to close the Attachments dialog box.

When you double-click the Attachment field, the Attachments dialog box opens, as shown in Exhibit 3-4. You can then open, save, or remove any attached files.

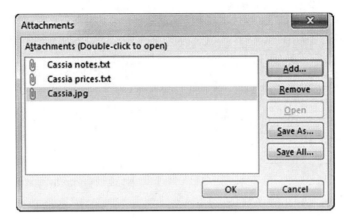

Exhibit 3-4: The Attachments dialog box

Do it!

A-4:   Using the Attachment data type

The files for this activity are in Student Data folder **Unit 3\Topic A**.

Here's how	Here's why
1 Select the row below sngMinQuantity	You'll add an Attachment field to this table.
Under Field Name, enter **atchDetails**	This field will store an image file and a text file for each product.
Under Data Type, select **Attachment**	
Under Description, enter **Photos and descriptions of product**	
2 In the Caption property box, enter **Details**	On the General tab in the Field Properties pane.
3 Update the table	You must update the table before you can switch views.
4 Switch to Datasheet view	

5	Observe the record for **Cassia**	The Details field displays a paperclip icon followed by a zero in parentheses. There are no files attached to this record.
6	Right-click within the Details field and choose **Manage Attachments...**	To open the Attachments dialog box.
	Click **Add**	The Choose File dialog box appears.
	Select **Cassia.jpg**	In the current topic folder.
	Hold down CTRL and select **Cassia notes.txt** and **Cassia prices.txt**	
7	Click **Open**	To close the Choose File dialog box. The three files are listed in the Attachments dialog box.
8	Click **OK**	To close the Attachments dialog box and add the three files to the record. The Details field now displays a 3 in parentheses to indicate that this record has three attachments.
	Double-click the field	To open the Attachments dialog box.
	Double-click **Cassia.jpg**	The image appears in the computer's default viewer application.
	Close the viewer	
9	Double-click **Cassia notes.txt**	The text appears in the computer's default text program.
	Close the text file	
10	Display **Cassia prices.txt**	The text in Cassia prices.txt is both redundant and out of date (the price has gone up). You'll delete this attachment to avoid confusing other users.
	Close the text file	
11	Click **Remove**	(In the Attachments dialog box.) To delete the attachment.
	Click **OK**	To close the Attachments dialog box.
12	Update and close the table	

Adding Totals rows

Explanation

You can add a Totals row at the bottom of a table to summarize its data. The fields in the Totals row can perform a variety of operations. When you insert a Totals row, a Total field appears at the bottom of each column in the table. For a numeric field, such as a Number or Currency data type, the Total field can perform the following operations:

- Sum
- Average
- Count
- Maximum
- Minimum
- Standard Deviation
- Variance

If the field is a non-numeric field, such as a short text or long text field, the total at the bottom can perform a Count of the number of records.

Do it!

A-5:   Adding a Totals row

Here's how	Here's why
1 Open tblEmployee in Datasheet view	You'll add a Totals row to this table.
Scroll to the bottom of the table	So that you can see the last row.
On the ribbon, click **Totals**	∑ Totals (In the Records group.) A Total row appears at the bottom of the table, below the New blank record row.
2 At the bottom of the EmpID column, click the **Total** field	A drop-down arrow appears.
Click the arrow	To display the list. Emp ID is an AutoNumber field, not a numeric field. The only options in the list are None and Count.
Select **Count**	This field now displays the number of employees in this table.
3 At the bottom of the Hire Date column, click the **Total** field and select **Minimum**	The hire date of the first employee hired appears.
4 Display the average employee salary	Click the field at the bottom of the Earnings column. From the list, select Average.
5 Update and close the table	
6 Close the database	

Topic B: Finding and editing records

This topic covers the following Microsoft Office Specialist exam objectives for Access 2013.

#	Objective
1.3	**Navigate through a Database**
1.3.1	Navigate to specific records
2.2	**Format a Table**
2.2.1	Hide fields in tables
2.3	**Manage Records**
2.3.1	Update records
2.3.5	Find and replace data

Finding and replacing values

Explanation

Scrolling through a large table to find specific records is not practical. Instead, you can use the Find feature to locate records that meet criteria you enter. You can also use Find to locate data values and replace them with different values. Using the Hide and Freeze Fields features also makes it easier to look through tables for what you need.

If you accidentally delete or change some values in a record when entering data, you can quickly restore the original values by pressing Ctrl+Z or by clicking Undo on the Quick Access toolbar.

To search for a value in a field:

1 Place the insertion point in the first data value in the specified field.
2 Click the Home tab (if necessary).
3 In the Find group, click Find to open the Find and Replace dialog box.
4 Specify criteria for the values you want to find.
5 Click Find Next.

The Find and Replace dialog box, shown in Exhibit 3-5, contains two tabs: Find and Replace. On the Find tab, you can specify criteria for the value you want to find. On the Replace tab, you can specify a value with which you want to replace it.

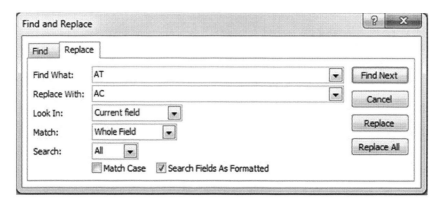

Exhibit 3-5: The Find and Replace dialog box

Wildcard searches

You can use wildcards to search for values in a field. A wildcard is a symbol that can represent any value, instead of a specific value. The asterisk (*) represents a string of any length, and the question mark (?) represents a single character. For example, searching a list of names for "Mar?" will return any four-letter string in which the first three characters are a match, such as Mark or Mary. Searching for "Mar*" will return strings of any length in which the first three characters match. In addition to Mark and Mary, it will return Marcus, Maria, and Martina.

Do it!

B-1:   Finding and replacing a value

The files for this activity are in Student Data folder **Unit 3\Topic B**.

Here's how	Here's why
1 Open Employees2	
2 Open tblEmployee in Datasheet view	(Double-click the table name in the Navigation Pane.) You'll find occurrences of the department code AT and replace them with AC.
3 Place the insertion point in the first data value in the Dept field	You'll search for a specific value in this field.
4 In the Find group, click **Find**

Find

(On the Home tab.) To open the Find and Replace dialog box. By default, the Find tab is active. |
In the Find What box, enter **AT**	To find this value in the Dept field.
In the Look In list, verify that **Current Field** is selected	To specify that the value is to be searched for in the Dept field.
In the Match list, verify that **Whole Field** is selected	To specify that the search needs to be done with the entire field.
In the Search list, verify that **All** is selected	To specify that the entire table needs to be searched.
Click **Find Next**	The first occurrence of AT, corresponding to the employee Shannon Lee, is highlighted.
5 Click the **Replace** tab	In the Find dialog box.
In the Replace With box, enter **AC**	

6	Click **Replace**	(To replace AT with AC.) The Dept entry for Shannon Lee changes to AC. The next occurrence of AT, corresponding to the employee Melissa James, is automatically highlighted.
	Click **Replace All**	To replace the remaining occurrences of AT without prompting for each one. A message box asks you to confirm the replace operation.
	Click **Yes**	To confirm that you want to do the replace, even though you won't be able to undo it.
7	Place the insertion point in the first data value in the Emp HR# field	You'll search for a specific value in this field.
	In the Find What box, enter **04***	To find all values beginning with 04.
	Click **Find Next**	The first occurrence of a number beginning with 04, corresponding to the employee Shannon Lee, is highlighted.
	Click **Find Next**	The next occurrence of a number beginning with 04, corresponding to the employee Annie Philips, is highlighted.
8	Find the remaining records	Click Find Next to highlight each record that begins with 04. When all records have been found, the Microsoft Office Access dialog box appears.
	Click **OK**	To close the dialog box.
9	Click **Cancel**	To close the Find and Replace dialog box.
	Observe the values in the Dept field	All five instances of AT have been replaced with AC.

Undoing changes in a table

Explanation   If you accidentally delete or modify a record, you can press Ctrl+Z to restore the deleted or modified values. You can also click Undo on the Quick Access toolbar. You can undo only the most recently changed value.

Do it!   ### B-2:   Undoing changes

Here's how	Here's why
1 In the Earnings column, select the first data value	
Press (DELETE)	To delete the value. You'll check whether this value can be restored.
2 Press (CTRL) + (Z)	To restore the deleted value.

Hiding and freezing fields

Explanation

Hiding fields temporarily removes them from view. This feature is useful if you want to focus on a smaller set of values. Freezing fields keeps them visible to the left of the datasheet window, even if you scroll to the right. For instance, if you have an employee table with many fields, you could freeze the Last Name and First Name fields so they remain visible as you scroll through the employee details.

To hide or freeze a field, right-click its column heading and choose Hide Fields or Freeze Fields. To hide or freeze several fields at once, select them; then right-click any selected column heading and choose Hide Fields or Freeze Fields.

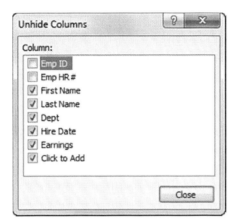

Exhibit 3-6: The Unhide Columns dialog box

To reverse the process, right-click any column heading and choose Unhide Fields or Unfreeze All Fields. The Unhide Fields command will open a dialog box, shown in Exhibit 3-6, in which you can specify which fields you want to be visible. You can use the Unhide Fields command to open this dialog box even if no fields are hidden.

Do it!   **B-3:   Hiding and freezing fields**

Here's how	Here's why
1 Click the column heading **Emp ID**	(TblEmployee should still be open in Datasheet view.) To select the whole column.
Hold (SHIFT) and click the column heading **Emp HR#**	To select this column also.
2 Right-click either selected column heading and choose **Hide Fields**	These fields are no longer visible.
3 Right-click any column heading and choose **Unhide Fields**	To open the Unhide Columns dialog box.
4 Check **Emp ID** and **Emp HR#**	To make them visible again.
5 Click **Close**	To close the dialog box and return to the table.
6 Right-click the column heading **Emp ID** and choose **Freeze Fields**	You need to shrink the window to see how this works, because this table is not very wide.
7 Resize the Access window so that you can't see the last two columns	You should still see the horizontal scrollbar.
Scroll left and right	The Emp ID field stays in place.
8 Right-click the column heading **Emp ID** and choose **Unfreeze All Fields**	
9 Close the database	Don't save any changes.

Topic C: Organizing records

This topic covers the following Microsoft Office Specialist exam objectives for Access 2013.

#	Objective
2.3	**Manage Records**
2.3.3	Delete records
2.3.6	Sort records
2.3.7	Filter records

Sorting and filtering

Explanation

You can organize records by sorting, filtering, and deleting them. *Sorting* is the process of organizing records in a meaningful way so that you can retrieve data in an order of your choice. For example, if you want to view records in ascending order of the last names of employees, you can sort the records based on the values in that field. You can sort records based on one or more fields.

Filtering records

Filtering is the process of temporarily isolating a subset of records that satisfy certain criteria you specify. For example, suppose that you want to delete or edit Human Resources department records in Datasheet view without navigating through the records of all the departments. To do this, you can filter the Human Resources department records to isolate them from the table containing the records of all the departments. You can also format and print the filtered records. Access provides several methods for filtering, such as Filter By Selection, Filter By Form, Filter Excluding Selection, and Advanced Filter/Sort.

When a colu nn is sorted, a small arrow appears in the field heading. When a column is filtered, a small filter symbol (a funnel) appears in the column heading.

Sorting records by a single field in a table

Records in a table are automatically sorted based on the primary key field. However, you might want to sort records based on a different field. The maximum number of characters for a sort field (or fields) is 255. You can sort in either ascending or descending order.

To sort a field in ascending order, select the field. In the Sort & Filter group on the Home tab, click Ascending or Descending. You can also right-click the field and choose Sort A to Z or Sort Z to A from the shortcut menu. In ascending sort order, text values will be sorted alphabetically from A to Z, and date values will be sorted from the earliest to the latest. Number or currency values will be sorted from the lowest value to the highest.

Removing a sort

To remove all sorts from a table, click Remove Sort in the Sort & Filter group on the Home tab. This button is enabled only if one or more columns are sorted.

Do it!

C-1:   Sorting records by a single field

The files for this activity are in Student Data folder **Unit 3\Topic C**.

Here's how	Here's why
1 Open Employees3	
2 Open tblEmployee	
3 Select the Last Name column, or put the insertion point anywhere in that column	You'll sort records in the Last Name field in ascending order.
4 In the Sort & Filter group, click ⬆ Ascending	(On the Home tab.) The records are sorted in ascending order based on the Last Name field.
Observe the Last Name column heading	There is an arrow to the right of the field name, indicating that there is a sort on that column.
Observe the Sort & Filter group	The Ascending button is highlighted, indicating that there is a sort on the table.
5 In the Sort & Filter group, click ⬆ Remove Sort	The Remove Sort button returns the records to their original order. The arrow in the column heading is gone, and the Ascending button is no longer highlighted.

Sorting records by multiple fields in a table

Explanation

You can sort records based on more than one field by selecting the fields and clicking the Ascending or Descending button in the Sort & Filter group on the Home tab. The fields must be adjacent to each other in Datasheet view. The sort fields have precedence from left to right. For example, if you select the fields Dept and Hire Date from left to right, the records will be sorted based first on Dept and then on Hire Date.

Selecting and sorting multiple fields

To select two fields, first click the field heading to select the first column. Then hold down the Shift key and select the other adjacent column. Both columns will be highlighted, as shown in Exhibit 3-7. Then sort the fields as necessary.

You can select more fields while holding down the Shift key, but if you select non-adjacent columns, all of the columns in between will also be selected. To sort by non-adjacent columns, just sort on one column and then the next; each sort will stay on the column until you clear it, with the most recent sort being the primary one.

You should also use this one-at-a-time method if you want to ensure that a certain column is sorted first, second, third, and so on. By default, when you select and sort by multiple columns, the leftmost column is the primary sort column. For instance, in Exhibit 3-7, if you were to select and sort by both First Name and Last Name, the records would sort primarily by the first name, so Adam, Anna, and Annie would be first. To sort primarily by the last name, you'd select and sort First Name, and then select and sort Last Name, because the most recent sort is the primary one.

First Name	Last Name	Dept	Hire Date	Earnings
Malcom	Pingault	SH	2/14/2001	$40,500.00
Shannon	Lee	AC	2/20/1998	$76,600.00
Melinda	McGregor	AD	5/5/2001	$30,200.00
James	Overmire	AD	9/19/1999	$87,000.00
Roger	Williams	MK	8/8/2002	$70,000.00
Annie	Philips	SH	9/12/2002	$31,000.00
Melissa	James	AC	3/1/2002	$53,500.00
Mary	Smith	AD	6/15/1989	$95,000.00

Exhibit 3-7: The tblEmployee table with two columns selected for sorting

Do it!   **C-2:   Sorting records by multiple fields**

Here's how	Here's why
1 Click the field heading **Dept**	To select this column.
2 Press and hold (SHIFT)	
Select the **Hire Date** column	Click the field heading. Both fields are selected.
Release (SHIFT)	
3 Click [A↓ Ascending]	(In the Sort & Filter group on the Home tab.) The records are sorted in ascending order, based first on Dept and then on Hire Date, because Dept is the leftmost sorted column. Small arrows appear in both field headings.
4 Click [A⁄Z Remove Sort]	(In the Sort & Filter group.) To clear the sorts.
5 Sort on First Name	Select the column and click Ascending. You'll sort by first and last name.
6 Sort on Last Name	Records are now sorted primarily by Last Name because that's the last field you sorted by.
7 Clear the sorts	Click Remove Sort.

Filtering records by using Filter By Selection

Explanation

In Datasheet view, you can use the Filter By Selection feature to display records based on a field value. For example, if you want to view the records of the Shipping department, you can apply a filter so that only records from the SH department appear in the table, as shown in Exhibit 3-8.

To filter records by using Filter By Selection, right-click the data value you want to filter and choose the appropriate option. You can also select the value and use the filter buttons in the Sort & Filter group on the Home tab. You can select a whole value or just part of it. For instance, if you select only the first letter of the last name "Jones" and then right-click the selection, the shortcut menu will include filter options for names beginning with "J."

Last Name	Dept	Hire Date	Earnings
Pingault	S	2/14/2001	$40,500.00
Lee	A	✂ Cut	$76,600.00
McGregor	A	🗐 Copy	$30,200.00
Overmire	A	🗐 Paste	$87,000.00
Williams	M		$70,000.00
Philips	SI	↓ Sort A to Z	$31,000.00
James	A	↓ Sort Z to A	$53,500.00
Smith	A	Clear filter from Dept	$95,000.00
Gregory	SI	Text Filters ▸	$30,000.00
Johnson	SI	Equals "SH"	$30,000.00
Anderson	SI		$29,900.00
Austin	M	Does Not Equal "SH"	$78,000.00
Roberts	SI	Contains "SH"	$30,000.00
Lee	SI	Does Not Contain "SH"	$30,000.00
Lawrence	SL	1/6/2001	$30,000.00

Exhibit 3-8: Filtering records from the shortcut menu

To remove a filter, click Toggle Filter in the Sort & Filter group, or right-click within the column and choose Clear Filters from the shortcut menu.

Do it!   **C-3:   Using Filter By Selection**

Here's how	Here's why
1 In the Dept column, select the value **SH** in the first record	You'll filter records for this value.
2 In the Sort & Filter group, click 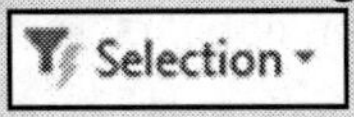 � **Selection ▾**	On the Home tab.
Observe the options	There are several for filtering with this value.
Click the button again	To close the menu without choosing an option.
3 In the Dept Column, right-click the value **SH**	To display the shortcut menu. It has the same filter options that you just saw.
Choose **Equals "SH"**	(As shown in Exhibit 3-8.) To filter out all records but those where Dept is equal to SH.
Observe the Dept field heading	It has a small filter symbol, indicating that a filter is active on that field.
4 Click **Toggle Filter**	(In the Sort & Filter group.) To remove the filter. The filter symbol no longer appears in the field heading.
5 In the Hire Date column, in the first record, select **2001**, as shown	Hire Date ▾ 2/14/2001
	Don't select the rest of the date. You'll filter to show only 2001 hires.
6 Right-click the selected text and choose **Ends With 2001**	The list is filtered by that year.
7 Right-click in the Hire Date column and choose **Clear filter from Hire Date**	(Right-click in the column but not on the heading.) This removes the filter from just the selected column, while the Remove Filter button removes all filters.

Filtering records by using Filter By Form

Explanation

The Filter By Form feature filters records based on a specific condition. When you use the Filter By Form feature in a table in Datasheet view, a table with empty fields appears. You can enter values in these empty fields to specify the filtering criteria.

To filter records by using Filter By Form:

1   In the Sort & Filter group, click Advanced to display a list.
2   Select Filter By Form. A blank form appears.
3   Enter criteria in the empty fields.

Do it!

C-4:   Using Filter By Form

Here's how	Here's why
1 In the Sort & Filter group, click **Advanced** and select **Filter By Form**	(On the Home tab.) A filter form opens.
2 In the first row, under Earnings, enter **>50000**, as shown	<table><tr><td>Hire Date</td><td>Earnings</td></tr><tr><td></td><td>>50000 ▾</td></tr></table> You'll display the records of employees whose earnings are greater than $50,000.
3 Click **Toggle Filter**	(In the Sort & Filter group.) The table now displays only the records of employees whose earnings are greater than $50,000.
4 Remove the filter	Click Toggle Filter.

Filtering records by using Filter Excluding Selection

Explanation

You use the Filter Excluding Selection feature to filter out (exclude) records containing a specific value. For example, you can use this feature to display the records of all employees except for those in the Accounting department.

To filter records by using Filter Excluding Selection, right-click a value you want to filter out and choose Does Not Equal <*value*> or Does Not Contain <*value*>.

Do it!

C-5:   Using Filter Excluding Selection

Here's how	Here's why
1 In the Dept column, right-click any **SL** value and choose **Does Not Equal "SL"**	You'll filter out all the people in the sales department.
2 Remove the filter	
3 Close the table	Do not save changes.

Filtering records by using Advanced Filter/Sort

Explanation   When you use the Advanced Filter/Sort feature, you specify the filtering criteria in a design grid. This feature helps you search for records that satisfy any specific or multiple criteria.

To filter records by using Advanced Filter/Sort, click Advanced in the Sort & Filter group and choose Advanced Filter/Sort to open the design grid. Then specify the criteria for filtering the records.

The design grid displays the selected table in the upper pane. In the lower pane, it displays columns in which you enter fields, and rows in which you specify sorting and filtering criteria, as shown in Exhibit 3-9.

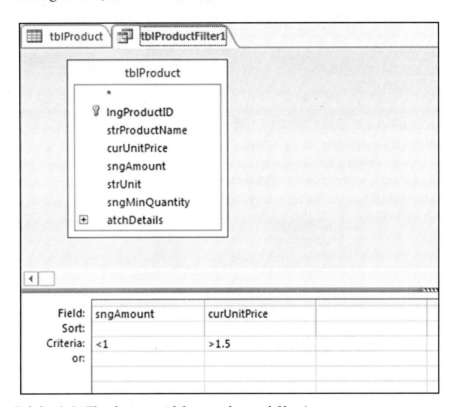

Exhibit 3-9: The design grid for an advanced filter/sort

Do it!

C-6: Using Advanced Filter/Sort

Here's how	Here's why
1 Open tblProduct	
2 Click **Advanced** and choose **Advanced Filter/Sort...**	(In the Sort & Filter group.) To open the design grid. The tblProduct table appears in the upper pane. The insertion point is in the first column of the field row in the lower pane.
3 In the Field row, select **sngAmount** from the list as shown	

Field:
Sort: | tblProduct.*
Criteria: | lngProductID
or: | strProductName
curUnitPrice
sngAmount
strUnit
sngMinQuantity
atchDetails

To add the sngAmount field to the design grid.

Place the insertion point in the second column of the Field row	You'll add a field to the second column of the Field row.
From the list, select **curUnitPrice**	To add this field to the design grid.
4 Place the insertion point in the first column of the Criteria row	You'll specify a criterion for the field sngAmount .
Enter **< 1**	To view the details of products with an amount of less than 1.
5 Place the insertion point in the second column of the criteria row	To specify a criterion for the field curUnitPrice.
Enter **> 1.5**	To view the details of products whose unit price is greater than $1.50.
6 Apply the filter	(Click the Toggle Filter button.) The table displays the records of the products whose current unit price is greater than $1.50 and whose amount is less than 1.
7 Remove the filter	

Deleting records

Explanation

To delete a record, select it. Then click Delete in the Records group, press the Delete key, or right-click and choose Delete Record. After a record is deleted, it cannot be restored.

Do it!

C-7: Deleting a record

Here's how	Here's why
1 Click as shown	(The tblProduct table is still open.) You'll delete a record in this table.
	2 Catnip Leaf
	➡ **3 Celery Seed (Whole)**
	4 Celery Seed (Ground)
	The third record contains the details for Celery Seed (Whole). A thick border now surrounds the record.
2 Click ✕ Delete	(In the Records group.) A message box appears, prompting you to confirm the deletion.
3 Click **Yes**	The record in the table is deleted.
4 Press (CTRL) + (Z)	It has no effect. You cannot undo the deletion of a record.
5 Close the table	No need to update—when you make changes to records in Datasheet view, the changes and the table are saved automatically.
6 Close the database	

Unit summary: Fields and records

Topic A   In this topic, you learned how to **modify the table design** by changing a field name and deleting, inserting, and moving fields. Then you learned how to **attach** a file to a record in a table. Finally, you learned how to create a **Totals row** for a table.

Topic B   In this topic, you learned how to use the **Find and Replace** dialog box to find and replace values in a table. You also learned how to **undo** changes made in a record. You then learned how to hide and **freeze fields**.

Topic C   In this topic, you learned how to **sort** records based on single or multiple fields. You also learned how to view selected records by applying a **filter**. You filtered records by using Filter By Selection, Filter By Form, Filter Excluding Selection, and Advanced Filter/Sort. Finally, you **deleted** a record.

Review questions

1 Which view is used to change the name of a field?

  A Design view   C Field view

  B Layout view   D Datasheet view

2 What is the first step before inserting or deleting a field?

3 By default, where are new rows inserted?

4 When you are deleting a field, in which of the following instance are you *not* prompted to confirm the deletion?

  A The field contains data.

  B The field is the primary key.

  C The table has not been saved since the field was added.

  D The field is a long text field.

5 What is the procedure to change a field name?

6 Which feature enables you to quickly locate records that meet specific criteria?

  A The Replace feature   C The Undo command

  B The scrollbar   D The Find feature

7 What is the difference between sorting and filtering?

8 Name some of the ways to filter records.

9 When you are sorting records by multiple fields, which sort field takes precedence in the sort?

10 True or false? Deleted records can be restored.

Independent practice activity

In this activity, you'll compare the design of two tables, and change one to match the other. Then you'll sort and filter records.

The files for this activity are in Student Data folder **Unit 3\Unit summary**.

1 Open RetailersIPA. Then open the table tblNewRetailer in Design view and observe its design.

2 Open the table tblRetailer in Design view and observe its design. Compare it to the design of tblNewRetailer.

3 Modify the design of the tblRetailer table so that it matches the tblNewRetailer table, as shown in Exhibit 3-10. Save the design changes. (*Hint:* First, edit the field names to match. Then, change the data types to match. Next, drag the fields so that their order matches. Insert a strFax field. Finally, add Descriptions.)

4 Save and close the tblRetailer table.

5 Switch to Datasheet view, and sort the records by First Name in ascending order.

6 Filter records to show only those records with a Region field equal to NY.

7 Remove the filter.

8 Use Filter By Form to show only records with a City value of Portland. (Hint: If necessary, remove "NY" from the form.)

9 Save and close the tblNewRetailer table.

10 Open the tblProduct table.

11 Use Advanced Filter/Sort to find products whose unit price is greater than $5.00.

12 Save and close the table and the database.

Field Name	Data Type	Description (Optional)
lngRetailerID	AutoNumber	Unique ID automatically assigned to each Retailer
strRetailerName	Short Text	Full name of Retailer
strAddr1	Short Text	Address Line 1 of Retailer
strAddr2	Short Text	Address Line 2 of Retailer
strCity	Short Text	Retailer's City
strRegion	Short Text	Retailer's State or Province (use std mailing abbreviation)
strPostalCode	Short Text	Retailer's Zip or Postal Code (use Zip+4 if possible)
strFirstName	Short Text	First name of purchasing agent at the Retailer
strLastName	Short Text	Last name of purchasing agent at the Retailer
strPhone	Short Text	Retailer's Voice Phone and extension
strFax	Short Text	Retailer's Fax number
lngRep	Number	Company Account Representative ID for this Retailer

Exhibit 3-10: The tblNewRetailer table design

Unit 4

Data entry rules

Complete this unit, and you'll know how to:

A Set properties for a field.

B Create input masks for fields, and use the Input Mask Wizard.

C Set validation rules for entering data in a field.

Topic A: Setting field properties

This topic covers the following Microsoft Office Specialist exam objectives for Access 2013.

#	Objective
2.2	**Format a Table**
2.2.2	Change data formats
2.4	**Create and Modify Fields**
2.4.4	Change field sizes
2.4.7	Set default values

Field properties

Explanation

You can set properties for the fields in a table to control how data is stored and displayed in that table. For example, you can ensure that the Product ID field is never left blank or that data in the Postal Code field contains only five digits. Field properties are set in the Field Properties pane in Design view.

You can set several properties for fields in a table. The following table describes some of these properties:

Property	Specifies
Required	The field cannot contain null values.
Allow Zero Length	The field can contain a blank, or a string of zero length.
Field Size	The maximum number of characters that can be entered in the field.
Append Only	The field can only be added to; existing data cannot be overwritten. (For Long Text fields only.)
Default Value	Data that is automatically entered for this field when a new record is created.

The Required property

The *Required* property ensures that a field does not contain a null value. (A *null value* indicates that nothing has been entered in the field.) If the Required property is set to Yes, you must enter a value in the field, *even if that value is a blank* (a blank is a string of zero length, and can be entered as ""). This prevents the field from being accidentally skipped over during data entry, but allows an intentionally blank value.

To set the Required property for a field:

1   Open the table in Design view.

2   Under Field Properties, display the General tab.

3   From the Required list, select Yes.

4   Update the table. A message box appears, stating that you can test the existing data for the new rule that you have set.

5   Click No to skip testing the current data against the new rule, or click Yes to test the data.

Note that the Required property might behave differently if the Allow Zero Length property is set. When you're using these properties, it is best to test different data values. Also, you might find that creating input masks and validation rules is more predictable than setting these properties.

Do it!   ## A-1:   Setting the Required property

The files for this activity are in Student Data folder **Unit 4\Topic A**.

Here's how	Here's why
1 Open Vendors1	In the current unit folder.
2 Open tblRetailer	
3 Click ⏭	(The Last record button is at the bottom of the tblRetailer window.) To move to the last record.
Under the Retailer Name column, enter **Magic Spices**	To specify the Retailer Name.
4 Click ⏭⁕	(The New (blank) record button is at the bottom of the tblRetailer window.) To add another record to this table. Notice that you have not entered data in any other fields in the record.
5 Switch to Design view	
6 Place the insertion point in the **strAddr1** field, as shown	

Field Name
lngRetailerID
strRetailerName
strAddr1

You'll set the Required property for the strAddr1 field. The general properties for this field appear on the General tab of the Field Properties pane.

7	Under Field Properties, on the General tab, from the Required list, select **Yes**, as shown	

Validation Text		
Required	No	
Allow Zero Length	Yes	
Indexed	No	
Unicode Compression	Yes	

		To set the Required field property.
8	Update the table	A data integrity message asks if you want the existing data to be tested against the new rule.
	Click **No**	To skip testing the data.
9	Switch to Datasheet view	You'll test the Required field property.
10	Add a new record	Click the New (blank) record button at the bottom of the tblRetailer window.
	Under Retailer Name, enter **Spice Outlet**	In the new record.
	Click	To add another new record. A message box warns you that you must enter a value in the strAddr1 field. This occurs because the Required property has been set for that field.
	Click **OK**	To close the message box. You'll enter a value in the Address1 field.
11	Press (TAB)	(If necessary.) To move to the Address1 cell.
	Enter **202 Brown St**	
12	Add a new record	The message box doesn't appear.
13	Delete the records for **Magic Spices** and **Spice Outlet**	
14	Set the Required property for strAddr1 back to **No**	If you don't, you'll be prompted to fill it in during all subsequent activities.
15	Update the table	

The Allow Zero Length property

Explanation

The *Allow Zero Length* can make a short text, long text, or hyperlink field accept strings of zero length (a blank or ""), which is sometimes necessary when you're importing data from other sources. Allow Zero Length will not flag a null value, because a null value is not a string of zero length.

You can set the Allow Zero Length property to No and set the Required property to Yes to ensure that the field cannot contain an empty string, a null value, or a space character, all of which would make the field appear blank. If you set the Allow Zero Length property to Yes, the field can contain values with no characters.

If Required is set to No and Allow Zero Length is set to Yes, only blank values will be flagged. Null values and spaces will get through. As noted earlier, validation rules and input masks, along with default values when appropriate, will often be more predictable.

To set the Allow Zero Length property for a field, display the General properties for the field. From the Allow Zero Length list, select Yes.

Do it!

A-2:   Using the Allow Zero Length property

Here's how	Here's why
1 Switch to Design view	If necessary.
Display the General properties for the strPhone field	(Under Field Name, place the insertion point in the field strPhone.) You'll set the Required and Allow Zero Length properties of this field.
From the Required list, select **Yes**	To set the Required property.
From the Allow Zero Length list, select **Yes**	To set the Allow Zero Length property.
2 Update the table	A message box appears, stating that Access can test the data in the table against the new rules.
Click **Yes**	To test the existing data and to save the table design.
3 Switch to Datasheet view	
4 Add a new record	
Under Retailer Name, enter **Magic Spices**	To specify the Retailer Name for the new record.
Under Address1, enter **111 SE Carnegie St**	
5 Under City, enter **Astoria**	Leave the Address2 field empty.
Under Region, enter **OR**	
Under Postal Code, enter **97102**	

6	Add a new record	A message appears, stating that you must enter a value in the strPhone field.
7	Click **OK**	To close the message box.
8	Place the insertion point in the Phone field	You'll enter a blank in this column.
	Enter **""**	(Two quotation marks with no space between.) You could also enter a space.
	Add a new record	The quotation marks do not remain because they are interpreted as a blank—a zero-length string. If time allows, experiment with how these properties accept or reject input.
9	Set the Required and Allow Zero Length properties back to **No**	
10	Update the table	If asked, do not check data validation rules.

The Field Size property

Explanation

The *Field Size* property specifies the maximum number of characters that can be entered in a field.

To set the Field Size property, display the General properties for the field you want. In the Field Size box, enter the desired field size.

Do it!

A-3:   Setting the Field Size property

Here's how	Here's why
1 Switch to Design view	If necessary.
Display the General properties for the field strPostalCode	
2 Edit the Field Size box to read **10**	To set the Field Size property for the field.
3 Update the table	A message box states that data might be lost because of the change in the Field Size property.
Click **Yes**	To save the table so that the current values of this field do not exceed five characters.
4 Switch to Datasheet view	
Navigate to the last record	(Click the Last record button at the bottom of the tblRetailer window.) You'll enter a postal code in this record.
5 In the Postal Code field in the last record, select the value as shown	TX 73344 OR 97102
Edit the field to read **97102-1234**	To enter a postal code in the U.S. Postal Service's ZIP + 4 format.
Edit the field to read **97102-12345**	Access will not allow you to type the last (11th) character because you set the Field Size property to 10.

The Append Only property

Explanation

For a long text field, the *Append Only* property keeps a history of all changes made in that field. You can view this history to see the date and time that changes were made, as well as the changes themselves.

To set the Append Only property, display the General properties for the long text field. Scroll down to the bottom of the list. From the Append Only list, select Yes.

To view the History, select any record in the changed column. Then right-click the changed field and choose Show Column History. A dialog box displays the changes, as shown in Exhibit 4-1.

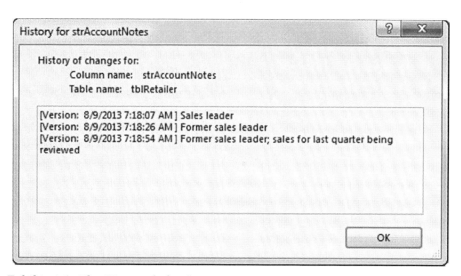

Exhibit 4-1: The History dialog box

If you later disable the Append Only property, all recorded history changes are deleted.

Do it!

A-4:   Setting the Append Only property

Here's how	Here's why
1 Switch to Design view	
2 Select any Short Text field	
Observe the General properties	The Append Only property is not listed. This property applies only to Long Text fields.
3 Display the General properties for the field strAccountNotes	
From the Append Only list, select **Yes**	To set the Append Only property.
4 Update the table	
Switch to Datasheet view	

5	Scroll to the right	To see the Account notes field.
	In the first record, type **Sales leader**	
	Press (↓)	Moving out of the field saves the change in the data value in the database.
6	Edit the first record to read **Former sales leader**	To change the long text field for this record.
	Press (↓)	To save the data value.
7	Edit the record to read **Former sales leader; sales for last quarter being reviewed**	
	Press (↓)	
8	Right-click the field you changed and choose **Show column history...**	The History for strAccountNotes dialog box appears.
	Observe the history	The date and time of the changes, as well as the changed text, are shown.
	Click **OK**	To close the dialog box.
9	Switch to Design view	
	For the strAccountNotes field, set Append Only to **No**	
10	Update the table	To save the changes in the design. A dialog box appears.
	Click **Yes**	To confirm that the history will be lost.
11	Switch to Datasheet view	
	In the Account notes column, right-click the changed record	The shortcut menu no longer includes Show Column History.

The Default Value property

Explanation

The *Default Value* property specifies data to be automatically entered in a field when a new record is created. This data value can be changed if necessary.

To set the Default Value property, display the General properties for the field you want. In the Default Value box, enter the data.

Do it!

A-5:   Setting the Default Value property

Here's how	Here's why
1 Switch to Design view	If necessary.
Display the General properties for the field strRegion	Most new customers are located in Oregon. You'll set that as the default value.
2 Edit the Default Value box to read **OR**	To set the Default Value property for the field.
Press [↵ ENTER]	The value changes to "OR". Access places quotes around the data string because this is a Short Text field.
3 Update the table	
4 Switch to Datasheet view	
Observe the last record	The Region field is already filled in.
5 In the Retailer Name field in the last record, enter **Spice Outlet**	Another New record is created, with OR as the Region field's default value.
Edit this record's Region field to read **TX**	To change the default value.
Press [TAB]	The default value has been replaced.
6 Close the database	

Topic B: Working with input masks

This topic covers the following Microsoft Office Specialist exam objectives for Access 2013.

#	Objective
2.4	**Create and Modify Fields**
2.4.8	Use input masks

Input masks

Explanation

An *input mask* defines how data should be entered in a field. It determines the type of data and the number of characters in it. For example, if you want all phone numbers in a table to contain only numerals and to appear in the same format, you can use an input mask such as (999) 999-9999.

The Format property defines the display format for a field or control. For example, you can format all dates in the month/day/year format or some other format. You can choose from a list of predefined formats for fields for the AutoNumber, Number, Currency, Date/Time, and Yes/No data types, or you can create your own custom format for any data type except OLE Object. The *OLE Object* data type is used to link to objects created in other applications, such as Microsoft Word.

Creating input masks

An input mask consists of *literals,* such as hyphens, underscores, or dashes, which separate blanks. Blanks are used as placeholders for data and are visible only in Datasheet view. The *Input Mask* property defines a field's input mask. For example, for the phone number input mask, you enter digits into the blanks.

An input mask definition contains three sections separated by semicolons:

- The first section contains the input mask. For example, the mask 000-000-0000 specifies that the field should contain 10 numerals with two separating hyphens.

- The second section specifies whether to store the literal characters that are entered in the field along with the characters that have been entered in the blanks.

  To define a literal character, enter any character other than the valid input-mask characters, including spaces and symbols. To define one of the valid input-mask characters as a literal character, precede that character with a backslash (\).

  If you specify 0 (zero) in the second section of the input mask, then both the literal characters and the values are stored. If you specify 1 or leave this section blank, only the values are stored. For example, for telephone number 555-333-4444, entering 0 in the second section stores 555-333-4444 in the field. Entering 1 in the second section stores 5553334444.

- The third section defines the characters that appear as placeholders for the blanks in the input mask. For example, if you specify * as a placeholder for the input mask 000-000-0000, then ***-***-**** appears in the field in the table's Datasheet view.

To create an input mask for a field:

    1 Open the table in Design view.

    2 Display the General properties.

    3 Click the Input Mask box.

    4 Enter the input mask.

    5 Update the table.

Input-mask characters

Access provides several input-mask characters and has specific interpretations for each one. A literal character must be preceded with a backslash (\). The following table lists some literal characters:

Character	Description
0 (zero)	The user must enter a numeral between 0 and 9.
9	The user can enter a numeral or a space, but entry is optional.
#	The user can enter a numeral or a space. Entry is optional, and all blank positions will be converted to spaces.
L	The user must enter a letter, A through Z.
?	The user can enter a letter, but entry is optional.
A	The user must enter either a letter or a numeral.
a	The user can enter a letter or a numeral, but entry is optional.
&	The user must enter any character or a space.
C	The user can enter a character or a space, but entry is optional.
<	Any letter that follows will be converted to lowercase.
>	Any letter that follows will be converted to uppercase.
Password	Setting the Input Mask property to the word Password creates a password entry text box. Any character typed in the text box is stored as the character but is displayed as an asterisk (*).

Do it!

B-1: Creating an input mask

The files for this activity are in Student Data folder **Unit 4\Topic B**.

Here's how	Here's why
1 Open Vendors2	
2 Open tblRetailer in Design view	
3 Display the General properties for the strPhone field	
4 In the Input Mask box, enter **(000) 000-0000 ?9999;0;#**	To set the Input Mask property. In the first section, the blanks begin with zeros, indicating that numerals are required. The last set of blanks begins with ?, calling for an optional letter. The ? is followed by 9999 for optional spaces or numerals. The second section contains 0, so the literal characters will be stored with the values. The # character in the third section is the placeholder for the blanks.
5 Update the table	If a smart tag appears for Property Update Options, ignore it.
6 Switch to Datasheet view	You'll test the input mask by entering sample data in the table.
7 In the last record, select the Phone field	
Observe the cell	(733) 220-1000 x4321 (336) 684-4700 (###) ###-#### ##### The # characters appear in the cell.
8 Select the first character and enter **ABC**	Nothing appears in the cell because the first characters in the string are required to be numerals.
Enter **5033051478x6485**	Notice that the # characters are replaced with the characters you enter.

The Input Mask Wizard

Explanation

You can use the Input Mask Wizard to create an input mask based on the built-in input masks in Access. To do so:

1 Open the table in Design view.

2 Display the general properties of the field that you want to set an input mask for.

3 Click the Input Mask box, and click the Build button to display the Input Mask Wizard.

4 From the Input Mask list, select the input mask you want. Click Next.

5 In the Input Mask box, change the input mask, if necessary.

6 From the Placeholder list, select a placeholder, if necessary.

7 Select the relevant option to specify whether you want to store the literal characters with the values entered in the blanks. Click Next.

8 Click Finish to create the input mask.

Do it!

B-2: Working with the Input Mask Wizard

Here's how	Here's why
1 In the Fax field, enter **5553334444**	This field does not contain an input mask.
2 Switch to Design view	
3 Display the General properties for the strFax field	You'll set an input mask for this field.
Click the Input Mask box	The Build button appears.
Click [...]	(The Build button is next to the Input Mask box.) To display the Input Mask Wizard.
4 In the list, verify that **Phone Number** is selected	
Click **Next**	To move to the next step of the wizard.
5 In the Input Mask box, edit **999** to read **000**	To make the area code required instead of optional.
6 In the Try It box, enter **5553334444**	The number appears in the input-mask format.
Click **Next**	To move to the next step of the wizard.

7 Select the first option, as shown

> How do you want to store the data?
>
> ◉ With the symbols in the mask, like this:
>
> (655) 337-0776
>
> ○ Without the symbols in the mask, like this:
>
> 04873813

You'll store both the literal characters and the values entered in the field.

Click **Next**

To move to the next step of the wizard.

8 Click **Finish**

To close the Input Mask Wizard and to set the input mask for the field.

Observe the Input Mask box

Input Mask	!\(000") "000\-0000;0;_

The exclamation mark in the input mask causes it to appear from right to left in Datasheet view. The blanks in the first section contain 0, so entering these values is required. The second section contains 0, so literals are stored with the values. The underscore in the last section (_) is the placeholder for the blanks.

9 Update the table

10 Switch to Datasheet view

In the last record, select the Fax field

To view the data in the input-mask format. The data in the Fax column now appears in the input-mask format.

11 Close the database

Topic C: Setting validation rules

This topic covers the following Microsoft Office Specialist exam objectives for Access 2013.

#	Objective
2.4	**Create and Modify Fields**
2.4.2	Add validation rules to fields

Validation rules

Explanation

You use a *validation rule* to check data that has been entered into a field. As with an input mask, you can set a format template that the data must match. With a validation rule, however, you can also use logical operators to check the data against multiple criteria. For instance, you can set a field to be in date format, and set it to reject dates later than the current day. If data entered in a field violates the validation rule, an error message appears and prompts for the correct value. You can set the text of the error message in the Validation Text property.

Following are some sample validation rules:

Rule	Description
Like "S???"	The value in the field must have four characters, and the first must always be S.
<>0	The value in the field must not be equal to zero (0).
0 or >100	The value in the field must be 0 or greater than 100.
<#1/1/2007	The date in the field must be earlier than January 1, 2007.

To create a validation rule, display the General properties of the field for which you want to set it. Then enter the rule in the Validation Rule box.

Do it!

C-1:   **Creating validation rules**

The files for this activity are in Student Data folder **Unit 4\Topic C**.

Here's how	Here's why
1 Open Vendors3	
2 Open tblProduct in Design view	
Display the General properties for the strUnit field	You'll set a validation rule for this field.
3 In the Validation Rule box, enter **Like "oz" Or Like "lb"**	To set the Validation Rule property. In the validation rule, "Like" is used to specify that the strUnit field should be entered in the format of the characters you specify after the word Like. This validation rule specifies that the values you enter in the field can only be either "oz" or "lb."
4 Update the table	A message box appears, asking if you want the existing data to be tested against the new rule.
Click **Yes**	To save the table's design and to test the existing data against the new validation rule.
5 Switch to Datasheet view	You'll try to change a value in the Unit field.
Navigate to the first record	
6 In the first record, change the value in the Unit field to **g**	For grams.
Press (TAB)	A message box appears, warning that the data you entered violates the field's validation rule.
Click **OK**	You'll enter the correct unit in this cell.
7 Change the Unit to **oz**	
Press (TAB)	No warning message appears.

The Validation Text property

Explanation

When you enter data that violates a field's validation rule, Access displays a message box. This message can be rather cryptic and hard to understand for the end-user, who might not know the underlying field names. You can set the *Validation Text* property to specify the error message in this message box.

To specify validation text for a field, display the General properties of the field. In the Validation Text box, enter the text that you want to display in the message box.

Do it!

C-2: Setting validation text

Here's how	Here's why
1 Switch to Design view	You'll specify the validation text for a validation rule so that the warning in the message box is easier to understand.
2 Display the General properties of the strUnit field	If necessary.
In the Validation Text box, enter **The values in the Unit field must be either "oz" or "lb"**	To set the Validation Text property for this field.
3 Update the table	
4 Switch to Datasheet view	You'll test the Validation Text property.
5 Navigate to the first record	You'll try to change the Unit for this record.
Change the Unit to **g**	
Press (TAB)	A message box appears, displaying the validation text you set.
6 Click **OK**	To close the message box. You'll enter the correct unit.
Change the Unit to **oz**	
7 Close the database	

Unit summary: Data entry rules

Topic A   In this topic, you learned how to set the **Required, Allow Zero Length, Field Size, Append Only**, and **Default Value** properties for a field. You learned that by setting these field properties, you can control how data is displayed and stored in a table.

Topic B   In this topic, you learned how to set an **input mask** for a field by entering the input mask in a field's Property Sheet. You learned that an input mask specifies the format for entering data in a field. You also learned how to set an input mask by using the **Input Mask Wizard**.

Topic C   In this topic, you learned how to set a **validation rule** for a field. In addition, you learned how to display customized messages by setting validation text.

Independent practice activity

In this activity, you will set a field's required property, create an input mask, and create a validation rule.

The files for this activity are in Student Data folder **Unit 4\Unit summary**.

1 Open ProductsIPA.

2 Set the Required property for the strProductName field of the tblProduct table to Yes.

3 Update and close the table.

4 Create an input mask for the strPhone field in the tblRetailer table. Edit the input mask to read **000\-000\-0000;1;***—this will ensure that only 10 numbers are entered in the field, and although the input mask will display numbers in a specific format in the table, only the numbers (not the literal characters) will be stored in the table. The asterisk (*) is used as a placeholder.

5 Update the table.

6 Test the input mask by entering sample data.

7 Close the table without saving.

8 Create a validation rule for the dtmOrderDate field in the tblOrder table to ensure that the dates entered are after 1/1/2013. (*Hint:* Enter the validation rule >#1/1/2013#.) Do not apply the rule to existing data. Set validation text for the rule.

9 Update the table.

10 Test the validation rule by entering sample data.

11 Close the table without saving. Then close the database.

Review questions

1 Which field property is used to specify that the field can contain null values?

   A Allow Zero Length   C Field Size

   B Required   D Format

2 Which field property is used to guarantee that a field does not appear blank? [Choose all that apply.]

   A Required   C Field Size

   B Allow Zero Length   D Format

3 What is the definition of a null value?

4 Describe the three sections of an input mask.

5 When you create an input mask, how do you indicate literal characters?

6 Identify the correct character for each of the following in an input mask:

Description	Character
The user must enter a number between 0 and 9.	
The user can enter a number (0–9) or a space, but entry is optional.	
The users must enter a letter, A–Z.	
The user can enter a letter (A–Z), but entry is optional.	
The user can enter a number or a space. Entry is optional, and all blank positions will be converted to spaces.	

7 Which field property is used to display a customized error message?

   A Default Value   C Validation Text

   B Validation Test   D Field Message Text

Unit 5

Basic queries

Complete this unit, and you'll know how to:

A Plan, create, save, and run queries; and use queries to sort data and to filter query results.

B Modify queries and query results by adding fields, and find records with empty fields.

C Perform operations in queries by using comparison operators; use AND and OR conditions in queries; and use expressions and aggregate functions.

Unit 5

Topic A: Creating and using queries

This topic covers the following Microsoft Office Specialist exam objectives for Access 2013.

#	Objective
3.1	**Create a Query**
3.1.1	Run queries
3.1.4	Create action queries
3.1.6	Save queries
3.2	**Modify a Query**
3.2.5	Sort data within queries

Using queries to retrieve data

Explanation

A *query* is a database object that retrieves and displays selective data from one or more tables or from other queries. For example, if you want to see all of the products with a unit price greater than $2, you can specify this condition in a query. Queries that select data based on specific criteria are also called *select queries*, as opposed to *action queries*, which do something like move or delete the selected records.

The results of a query are displayed in Datasheet view. The result fields in a query datasheet use the formats and properties set in the base table. You can edit, navigate, sort, and filter these results just as you would in a table in Datasheet view. A *filter* is a set of conditions applied to data to view a section of data. Query results are similar to the results of a filter, but a query is a database object that you can save permanently, whereas a filter provides only a temporary view.

To extract data by using a query, you need to plan and define the following:

- The conditions that you want the data to meet
- The fields that you want to see in the query result
- The tables from which you'll extract the fields
- The statements that you'll use to extract data

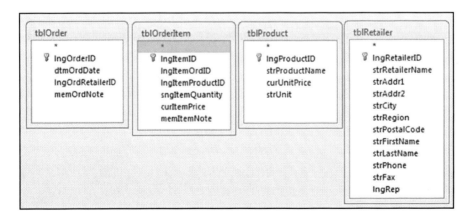

Exhibit 5-1: Tables open in query Design view

Do it! **A-1: Planning a query**

Questions and answers

You have designed a database containing the tables shown in Exhibit 5-1. With respect to these tables, answer the following:

1 You need to extract product details for all records with a unit price greater than $3. To what field would the condition apply?

2 You want to display the details of the retailers in a specific city that is in a specific region. To what fields would this condition apply, and from which table would you extract this information?

3 What fields would you want to display when you run the query to display records with a unit price greater than $3?

Basic queries

Explanation You can use the Query Wizard to retrieve data from one or more tables or queries:

1 Switch to Datasheet view (if necessary).

2 Click the Create tab.

3 In the Macros & Code group, click the Query Wizard button.

4 In the New Query dialog box, select Simple Query Wizard and click OK to open the first page of the Simple Query Wizard, shown in Exhibit 5-2.

5 From the Tables/Queries list, select the table that you want to base the query on.

6 From the Available Fields list, select the fields for the query, and add them to the Selected Fields list. Click Next to move to the next page of the wizard.

7 Select the relevant option to display either detailed results or a summary of the query result. (This wizard page will appear only if you select a numeric field for your query.) Click Next. In the "What title do you want for your query?" box, enter a title for the query.

8 Select the option to either open the query or modify its design. Click Finish to exit the wizard and create the query.

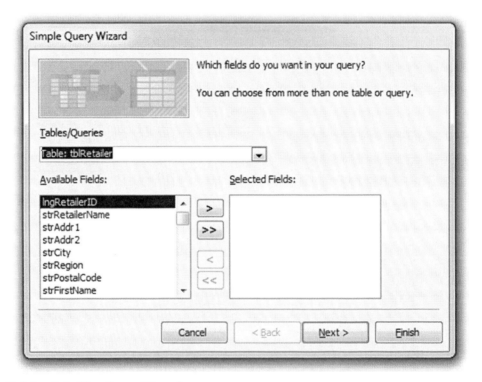

Exhibit 5-2: The Query Wizard

Do it!

A-2: Using the Query Wizard

The files for this activity are in Student Data folder **Unit 5\Topic A**.

Here's how	Here's why
1 Open the database Operations1	You'll create a query to view the names and addresses of the retailers from the tblRetailer table.
2 Click the **Create** tab	
3 In the Queries group, click **Query Wizard**	To open the New Query dialog box.
4 In the dialog box, select **Simple Query Wizard**	(If necessary.) You'll use the wizard to create a query.
Click **OK**	To open the Simple Query Wizard.
5 From the Tables/Queries list, select **Table: tblRetailer**	You'll create the query based on this table. The fields of the selected table, tblRetailer, appear in the Available Fields list, shown in Exhibit 5-2.
6 Click >>	To add all of the fields from tblRetailer to the query. The entire contents of the Available Fields list moves to the Selected Fields list. You'll change this to use only selected fields from the table.
Click <<	To move all of the fields back to the Available Fields list.
7 From the Available Fields list, select **strRetailerName**	
Click >	(The Add button.) To add the field to the Selected Fields list.
Add **strAddr1** to the Selected Fields list	Select the field in the Available Fields list and click the Add button.
Click **Next**	To move to the next page of the wizard.

8	Edit the "What title do you want for your query?" box to read **qryRetailerDetails**	This will be the title of the query.
	Verify that the first option is selected, as shown	⦿ Open the query to view information. ○ Modify the query design.
		You'll view the query results as soon as you finish creating the query.
9	Click **Finish**	To view the query results in Datasheet view.
	Observe the results of the query	The retailers' names and addresses appear in the query result. By default, the record selector is on the first record.
10	Close the query	
11	From the Navigation Pane menu, choose **All Access Objects**	(If necessary.) To display the new query in the Navigation Pane. You can double-click the query any time you want to run it. A query refers to its source tables every time it is run and will reflect the latest changes in the tables.

Creating queries in Design view

Explanation

You can use Design view to create or modify queries. For basic queries, Design view contains a design grid in the lower pane, as shown in Exhibit 5-3. In the upper pane, Design view contains the field list for the table or tables on which the query is based. A field list displays all of the fields in the record source. To create a query, you must select one or more data sources and define the specifications of the query in Design view. The sources for the queries can be other queries or tables.

To create a basic query in Design view:

1 Open the database.
2 On the Create tab, click Query Design.
3 In the Show Table dialog box, select the table you want to add to the query, and click Add.
4 Click Close to return to Design view.
5 Select the fields that you want to display in the query results. Apply any sorts or criteria to the fields.
6 Click the Run button or switch to Datasheet view to see the query results.

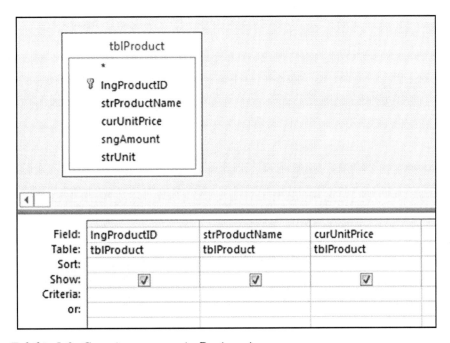

Exhibit 5-3: Creating a query in Design view

A-3: Creating a query in Design view

Here's how	Here's why
1 On the Create tab, click **Query Design**	To open a new query in Design view and open the Show Table dialog box.
2 Verify that the Tables tab is active	In the dialog box.
3 Select **tblProduct**	The query will be based on this table.
Click **Add**	To add the table to the upper pane in Design view.
Click **Close**	To close the Show Table dialog box.
4 Observe Design view	The upper pane displays the field list for the tblProduct table.
5 In the lower pane of the design grid, verify that the insertion point is in the first cell of the Field row	You'll enter a field here.
6 Display the field list in the first cell of the Field row	tblProduct.* lngProductID strProductName curUnitPrice sngAmount strUnit The field list contains the table name with an asterisk (*) and the names of all fields in the table.
7 From the field list, select **tblProduct.***	To add all fields in the table to the query.
Observe the design grid	Field: tblProduct.* Table: tblProduct Sort: Show: ☑ Criteria: or: Adding the table name with its asterisk adds all fields in that table. You'll change the query so it uses only selected table fields.

8	From the field list, select **lngProductID**	To add this field to the design grid.
	Observe the design grid	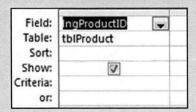

		The design grid displays lngProductID in the first cell of the Field row; tblProduct appears in the Table row; and the checkbox in the Show row is checked. This indicates that the field lngProductID will appear in the query result.
9	In the upper pane, in the table field list, double-click **strProductName**	This is another way to add fields to the query.
10	Add **curUnitPrice** to the design grid	Double-click it in the upper pane, or select it from the third field list in the lower pane.
	Observe the design grid	The design grid displays the fields lngProductID, strProductName, and curUnitPrice, as shown in Exhibit 5-3. These three fields will appear in the query results.

Saving and viewing query results

Explanation

You can save a query by clicking the File tab and choosing Save Object As, or by clicking the Save button on the Quick Access toolbar. If you try to close an unsaved query, you'll be asked if you want to save it.

To see the results of the query, you must run it. To run the query, click Run in the Results group on the Query Tools | Design tab, or just switch to Datasheet view. The results of a query are shown in Exhibit 5-4.

qryPrices		
Product ID ▾	Product Name ▾	Unit Price ▾
1	Cassia	$3.00
2	Catnip Leaf	$2.75
3	Celery Seed (Whole)	$1.75
4	Celery Seed (Ground)	$1.50
5	Chamomile Flowers	$1.00

Exhibit 5-4: Query results

Do it!

A-4: Saving and running the query

Here's how	Here's why
1 On the Quick Access toolbar, click 🖫	When you click this button to save a new object, the Save As dialog box opens. After that, clicking the button updates the object.
2 Edit the query name to read **qryPrices**	
Click **OK**	To save the query with the specified name. The tab of the Design window displays the name qryPrices, and the name appears in the Navigation Pane.
3 In the Results group, click **Run**	! Run
	(On the Query Tools | Design tab.) The results window appears. The fields Product ID, Product Name, and Unit Price appear in Datasheet view, as shown in Exhibit 5-4. The record selector is on the first record.

Sorting query results in Design view

Explanation

Sorting refers to organizing records in either ascending order or descending order based on the contents of a field. You can sort query results in the same way that you sort records in a table. The sort order is evaluated from left to right. The left sort field is the primary sort field. You can save the sort order with the query object. If you do not specify any sort order, the records are sorted by the table's primary-key field.

To sort records in a query:

1 In the design grid, place the insertion point in the preferred cell of the Sort row. A drop-down arrow appears on the right side of the cell.

2 Display the Sort list and select a sort order.

3 Run the query.

Do it!

A-5:   Sorting query results

Here's how	Here's why
1 Switch to Design view	
2 Place the insertion point in the third column of the Sort row	(Under curUnitPrice.) To sort the records based on the field curUnitPrice.
3 Display the Sort list, as shown	curUnitPrice tblProduct Ascending Descending (not sorted)
4 Select **Descending**	To arrange the records in descending order of curUnitPrice. In the third cell of the Sort row, Descending is selected.
5 Run the query	Click the Run button or switch to Datasheet view.
Observe the results	The records in the query results are sorted based on the descending order of the values in the Unit Price field.

Specifying criteria to filter queries

Explanation

You can filter records by specifying criteria. You use criteria to specify a condition in the design grid to display specific records. For example, you can specify criteria to view the products sold on a specific date, or view the products whose unit price is greater than a specific value, or view the records that contain a specific value for a specific field. To add a criterion to a query, enter it in the Criteria row, and run the query.

Do it!

A-6: Filtering a query by adding criteria

Here's how	Here's why
1 Switch to Design view	You'll specify a query criterion for the field lngProductID.
2 Place the insertion point in the third cell of the Criteria row	
3 Enter **>1.5**	This query criterion will display details about products with a unit price greater than $1.50.
4 Run the query	
Observe the query result	It shows details for products whose unit price is higher than, but not equal to, $1.50.
Update and close the query	

Creating queries from filters

Explanation   When you filter a table, you can save the filter as a query. The results of the query are the same as the results of the filter.

To create a query from a filter:

1   Filter a table according to any desired criteria.

2   Click the File tab and click Save Object As.

3   In the Save As dialog box, enter a name and select Query from the As list. Then click OK.

Do it!   ## A-7:   Creating a query from a filter

Here's how	Here's why
1 Open tblEmployee	You'll filter the data in this table and then create a query from that filter.
2 Place the insertion point in the first record in the Earnings column	
Click **Filter**	(On the Home tab.) The Filter menu appears.
3 Choose **Number Filters, Greater Than...**	To open the Custom Filter dialog box.
In the "Earnings is greater than or equal to" box, enter **40000**	You'll filter the employees by those who earn more than $40,000.
Click **OK**	To close the dialog box and filter the table. The number of records displayed is reduced.
4 On the File tab, click **Save As**	
On the Save As page, click **Save Object As**	
Click	To open the Save As dialog box.

Save As

5 Edit the "Save 'tblEmployee' to" box to read **qryEmp40k**	The new query appears.
From the As list, select **Query**	Save 'tblEmployee' to: qryEmp40k As Query
	To save this as a query.
Click **OK**	The query displays.
6 Observe the number of records in the query	(Look at the status bar at the bottom of the window.) There are 15 employees who earn at least $40,000.
Close the query	
7 In tblEmployee, clear the filter	Click Toggle Filter on the Home tab.
In record 3, edit Melinda McGregor's earnings to read **$40,200.00**	To change her salary from $30,200 to $40,200.
Click anywhere in the table	To save the change in that record.
8 Run **qryEmp40k**	Double-click the query in the Navigation pane.
Observe the number of records	This query now returns 16 records instead of 15.
Observe the third record	Melinda McGregor is now included in the query results.
9 Close the table and the query	Don't save changes.
10 Close the database	

Topic B: Modifying query results and queries

This topic covers the following Microsoft Office Specialist exam objectives for Access 2013.

#	Objective
3.2	**Modify a Query**
3.2.2	Add new fields
3.2.3	Remove fields
3.2.4	Hide fields

Modifying queries

Explanation

Queries are not just data to look at—you can edit the results of a query, and the corresponding data will change in the query's source tables. You can modify the query itself any time by returning to Design view.

Editing query results in Datasheet view

Unlike data in a static report, the data in a query are still connected to their source tables. If you change the records shown in the query result, those changes are reflected in the table on which the query is based. To edit a record in a query result, enter the new values in Datasheet view and save the query result. You can then open the source table to view the edited values.

Do it!

B-1: Editing query results

The files for this activity are in Student Data folder **Unit 5\Topic B**.

Here's how	Here's why
1 Open Operations2	
2 Run qryPrices	You'll edit the query results.
In the query table, change Unit Price of Chives (Bulk) to **15**	This will be the new value for the Unit Price. You don't need to add the dollar sign.
Update the query	Updating the query also updates the table on which the query is based.
3 Close the query	Save changes if prompted.
4 Open tblProduct in Datasheet view	(Double-click it in the Navigation Pane.) You'll check whether the value you changed in the query result is reflected in the source table.
Observe the record for Chives (Bulk)	The Unit Price for this product is now $15.00. The value modified in the query result is reflected in the source table.
5 Close the table	

Modifying the query design

Explanation

To edit a query, open it in Design view. You can hide, move, add, and remove fields, change sorting parameters, and add criteria.

- To hide a field, clear the checkbox in the Show row. This is useful if you want to use a given field for criteria, but don't want it to show in the query results.

- To move a field column, first select it, and then drag the top of the column to where you want it. You select the column by clicking the very top, just above the field row.

- To remove a field from a query, place the insertion point in any row in the field column, and click Delete Columns. You can also select the field column and press Delete.

Do it!

B-2: Adding and removing fields in a query

Here's how	Here's why
1 Open qryPrices in Design view	You'll modify your earlier query by adding the field sngAmountt to it.
2 Delete **>1.5** from the Criteria row	To delete the criterion set to display only products with a unit price over $1.50.
3 Select the first column	Point to the top of the column, just above the field row, and click. The whole column will be selected.

Drag the top of the first column to the right of the second column

Field:	lngProductID	strProductName	curUnitPrice
Table:	tblProduct	tblProduct	tblProduct
Sort:			Descending
Show:	☑	☑	☑
Criteria:			
or:			

	To move it in the layout. Now the name will appear first in the query.
4 Place the insertion point in the fourth cell of the Field row	You'll add another field to the query.
5 In the field list, double-click **sngAmount** and **strUnit**	To add these fields to the query.
6 Run the query	The query result now contains two additional fields: Amount and Unit.
7 Switch to Design view	
8 In the Show row of the **lngProductID** column, clear the checkbox	It won't appear in the query results, even if you use it to match criteria.
9 Click in any field in the **strUnit** column	
Click **Delete Columns**	To remove the field from the query.
10 Run the query	Three columns are shown in the result. You hid one field and removed the other.

Records with empty fields

Explanation

An empty field sometimes causes problems in a table. For example, if you want to multiply values in the fields Quantity and Price Paid, and one of these fields does not contain a value, you'll get an incorrect result. You might want to display or remove fields that don't contain values. Unknown (empty) values in fields are referred to as *null* values. Null values cannot be entered in the primary-key field, nor can they be used in calculations. You can specify Is Null in the field criteria to find all records where no entry has been made in a specific field.

To search for records that contain null values, enter "Is Null" in the specific cell in the Criteria row, and run the query.

Do it!

B-3: Finding records with empty fields

Here's how	Here's why
1 Switch to Design view	
2 Add strUnit back in the query	Place the insertion point in the fifth cell of the Field row. Double-click strUnit in the field list.
3 Place the insertion point in the fourth cell of the Criteria row	(Under sngAmount.) You'll search for records that do not have any values in the sngAmount field.
4 Enter **Is Null**	This criterion ensures that records with null values in the sngAmount field appear in the query results.
5 Run the query	A record with an empty Amount field appears.
6 Close the database	Don't save changes.

Topic C: Performing operations in queries

This topic covers the following Microsoft Office Specialist exam objectives for Access 2013.

#	Objective
3.3	**Utilize Calculated Fields and Grouping within a Query**
3.3.1	Add calculated fields
3.3.3	Group and summarize data
3.3.4	Use comparison operators
3.3.5	Use basic operators

Creating calculated fields

Explanation

You can perform comparison operations or calculations by using queries. To view records based on multiple conditions, you use the comparison operators to add criteria to a query. To create a query containing multiple criteria, use the AND condition or the OR condition. You can also add a specific criterion in the query for a text field by using a wildcard operator.

You can perform calculations on field values. For example, you can calculate discounts for products based on values in the Unit Price field in the tblProduct table. To calculate values based on the fields in a table, you don't need to add a new field to the table to store the calculated values. Instead, you can use a query object to create a calculated field from the data in the source table. The calculated values are not stored in the source table, so they do not require more computer memory space. Calculations are performed each time the query is run, so the calculated field always contains the latest value. To perform calculations on a group of records, you can use aggregate functions, such as Sum, Avg, Count, or Min, in Design view.

Comparison operators

You use a comparison operator in a query to find records with matching values in one or more fields. A comparison operator is a symbol such as > (greater than) or < (less than). For example, you can search for all records with a unit price greater than (>) 2.35.

Comparison operators also specify a condition for a query. To use a comparison operator, place the insertion point in the proper cell of the Criteria row. Enter the criterion by using a comparison operator, and run the query.

The following table lists the comparison operators:

Operator	Description
>	Greater than
<	Less than
=	Equal to
<=	Less than or equal to
>=	Greater than or equal to
<>	Not equal to

Do it!

C-1: Using comparison operators

The files for this activity are in Student Data folder **Unit 5\Topic C**.

Here's how	Here's why
1 Open Operations3	
2 Open qryPrices in Design view	
3 Delete the previous criterion	(Select Is Null and press Delete.) You'll edit this query to specify a criterion using a comparison operator.
4 Place the insertion point in the third cell of the Criteria row	
5 Enter **>2.3**	To enter a query for viewing the details of products whose unit price is greater than $2.30.
6 Run the query	The records with a unit price greater than $2.30 appear in the result.

OR conditions

Explanation

You can specify two conditions in the criteria and display the records that satisfy either condition. For example, you might want to see records whose unit price is greater than $2 or whose unit value is equal to 2 oz. To display these records, you can use an OR condition for specifying the criteria.

To filter query results with the OR condition, enter the condition in the proper cell(s) of the row in the design grid, and run the query.

Do it!

C-2: Using the OR condition

Here's how	Here's why
1 Switch to Design view	
2 Delete the previous criterion	
3 Place the insertion point in the third cell of the Criteria row	(If necessary.) You will enter a criterion for the field curUnitPrice.
4 Enter **>2**	You want to find records with a unit price greater than $2.00.
5 Place the insertion point in the fourth cell of the "or" row	Under sngAmount.
6 Enter **>1.5**	This will be the criterion for sngAmount.
7 Run the query	Products appear that have either a unit price greater than $2.00 or a unit value greater than 1.5 oz, or both.

AND conditions

Explanation

When you use more than one condition in a query, you might want the query result to show the records that satisfy all of the conditions. For example, you can search for products with a unit price greater than $1.40 and less than $1.90. Here, you can use the AND condition. The query result will show only the records that satisfy both conditions.

To use an AND condition, enter it in the proper cell of the Criteria row, and run the query.

Do it!

C-3: Using the AND condition

Here's how	Here's why
1 Switch to Design view	
2 Delete both previous criteria	
3 Place the insertion point in the third cell of the Criteria row	(If necessary.) You'll enter a criterion for curUnitPrice.
4 Enter **>1.4 and <1.9**	
5 Run the query	

Product Name	Unit Price	Amount	Unit
Carob Powder (Raw)	$1.89	1.5	oz
Basil Leaf (Whole)	$1.89	3	oz
Celery Seed (Whole)	$1.75	1	oz
Celery Seed (Ground)	$1.50	1	oz
Anise Seeds	$1.49	2.5	oz
Asafoetida Powder	$1.49	0.5	oz
Basil Leaf (Ground)	$1.45	2	oz

The results show those products that have a unit price greater than $1.40 and less than $1.90.

Wildcard operators

Wildcard operators are used to retrieve multiple values. For instance, you might be looking for records that start with a certain letter or letters. You can use a wildcard operator to specify your criteria. *Wildcards* are operators that you can use as placeholders.

Two frequently used wildcard operators are the question mark (?) and the asterisk (*). The question mark is used to substitute for a single character. The asterisk is used to substitute for any number of characters.

For example, if you set the criterion on a First Name field to A*, a query would return all names beginning with A. If you set the criterion to A??, you would get Ann and Amy, but not Alex or Atoz, because each question mark specifies a single character. Only three-letter names that start with A would be returned.

When you use an asterisk in the criterion, Access inserts a Like operator and surrounds the character and the * with double quotation marks. A Like operator is used to search for specific text.

C-4:   Using the * wildcard

Here's how	Here's why
1 Switch to Design view	
2 Delete the previous criterion	
3 Place the insertion point in the second cell of the Criteria row	(Under strProductName.) You'll use a wildcard operator.
4 Enter **A***	To search for all products whose names start with A.
Press (TAB)	To move to the next cell. The criterion under strProductName changes to Like "A*".
5 Run the query	The results show details for only the products whose names start with A.

Using calculations

Explanation

An *expression* is a combination of symbols—identifiers, operators, and values—that produces a result. An expression can include the normal arithmetic operators for addition (+), subtraction (-), multiplication (*), and division (/). When creating a calculated field, you must enclose field names referenced in an expression in square brackets.

To use calculations in a query, enter the expression in the proper cell of the Field row, and run the query.

Product Name ⯆	Unit Price ⯆	Amount ⯆	Unit ⯆	Discount ⯆
Chives (Bulk)	$17.00	1	lb	1.7
Cinnamon Ground (Bulk)	$14.89	1	lb	1.489
Carob Pods	$12.49	6	oz	1.249
De Arbol Peppers (Whole)	$5.50	2	oz	0.55
De Arbol Pepper (Ground)	$4.25	2	oz	0.425
Chinese Star Anise (Ground)	$3.50	0.5	oz	0.35
Cassia	$3.00	2	oz	0.3
Catnip Leaf	$2.75	2.25	oz	0.275
Caraway Seed	$2.50	2.5	oz	0.25
Cinnamon Ground	$2.29	2	oz	0.229
Chili Pepper Powder	$2.00	2.25	oz	0.2

Exhibit 5-5: Query results from calculations

Do it!

C-5:   Using calculations in a query

Here's how	Here's why
1 Switch to Design view	
2 Delete the previous criterion	
3 Place the insertion point in the sixth cell of the Field row	You will enter an expression to calculate a discount.
4 Enter the following code: `Discount:[curUnitPrice]*0.1`	 To calculate the discount as 10% of the Unit Price. Here, the calculated field is Discount.
5 Run the query	The results appear, as shown in Exhibit 5-5. A new field, Discount, appears. This field contains the calculated discount values.
6 Update and close the query	

Calculating totals

Explanation

You can perform calculations on groups of records instead of on single records. For example, while viewing a set of records containing information about products sold in each order, you can view the total sales of these same products. To calculate values for a group of records, you can use *aggregate functions* by adding the values to the Total row of the query design grid. The Total row appears in the design grid when you click the Totals button in the Show/Hide group on the Query Tools | Design tab.

You use the Sum aggregate function to total the values for a field. The Max and Min aggregate functions are used to find the maximum and minimum values of a field. You can use the Group By calculation to group records based on similar field values.

Do it!

C-6:   Totaling a group of records

Here's how	Here's why
1 Open **tblOrderItem**	
Observe the table	You'll calculate the total paid for each order. Several records contain the same value for Order ID, meaning that they were part of the same order. You can create a query to total the values in the field Price Paid grouped by Order ID.
2 Click the **Create** tab	
3 In the Macros & Code group, click **Query Design**	To start a new query in Design view and open the New Query dialog box. You'll use the new query to total the values in the field curItemPrice grouped by lngItemOrdID.
4 Add **tblOrderItem** to the query	In the Show Table dialog box, select tblOrderItem, click Add, and click Close.
5 Add the fields **lngItemOrdID** and **curItemPrice** to the Field row	
6 In the Show/Hide group, click **Totals**	(On the Query Tools | Design tab.) The Total row appears, and Group By appears in that row.
Place the insertion point in the second cell of the Total row	

7	Display the Total list	
8	From the list, select **Sum**	To calculate the sum of the values in the field curItemPrice.
9	Run the query	

Order ID	SumOfcurItemPrice
1	$12.75
2	$5.25
3	$1.00
4	$22.29

The heading Price Paid changes to SumOfcurItemPrice. Under this heading, the sum of the price paid in each order appears.

10	Save the query as **qryTotals**
11	Close the query
	Close the table

The Avg and Count functions

Explanation

You use the Avg aggregate function to find the average of the values in a field for a group of records. For example, you can calculate the average sales of each product.

To find the number of values in a field, you use the Count aggregate function. For example, you can find out the number of products having the same unit price. The Count function does not count fields with null (blank) values.

Do it!

C-7: Using the Avg and Count functions

Here's how	Here's why
1 Create a new query in Design view	(On the Create tab, click Query Design.) You want to find the average sales of each product.
2 Add **tblOrderItem** to the query	Add the table and close the Show Table dialog box.
3 Add these fields to the Field row: **lngItemProductID** and **sngItemQuantity**	
4 Add the Total row	Click Totals in the Show/Hide group.
5 From the Total list under the field sngItemQuantity, select **Avg**	You'll calculate the average quantity sold for each product.
6 Run the query	The average quantity sold for each product appears under the heading AvgOfsngItemQuantity.
7 Switch to Design view	
8 Place the insertion point in the first cell of the Total row	(Under lngItemProductID.) You'll now find the number of products sold in each order.
From the Total list, select **Count**	To calculate the total number of values in the field lngItemProductID.
9 Place the insertion point in the second cell of the Field row	
From the field list, select **lngItemOrdID**	You'll find the number of products sold in each order.
10 Under lngItemOrdID, from the Total list, select **Group By**	This will group the records with the same Order ID.
11 Run the query	The number of products sold for each order appears under the heading CountOflngItemProductID.
12 Save the query as **qryCalculations**	

The Min and Max functions

Explanation   The Min and Max aggregate functions return the smallest and largest values in a field.

Do it!   **C-8: Using the Min and Max functions**

Here's how	Here's why
1 Switch to Design view	You'll edit the query to find the maximum and minimum amounts sold for each product.
2 Place the insertion point in the second cell of the Field row	
From the field list, select **sngItemQuantity**	You'll find the number of products sold in each order.
From the Total list, select **Max**	To calculate the maximum value in the field sngItemQuantity.
3 Place the insertion point in the first cell of the Total row	Under lngItemProductID.
From the Total list, select **Group by**	This will group the records with the same Product ID.
4 Run the query	The maximum amount of each product sold appears under the heading MaxOfsngItemQuantity.
5 Switch to Design view	You'll query for the minimum amount.
Under sngItemQuantity, from the Total list, select **Min**	
Run the query	The minimum amount of each product ordered appears. (In cases where a product was ordered only once, the maximum amount and the minimum amount are the same.)
6 Update and close the query	
Close the database	

Unit summary: Basic queries

Topic A   In this topic, you learned how to plan and create a **query**. You created queries by using the Query Wizard and Design view. You saved and ran a query. You also **sorted** and **filtered** records in the query datasheet.

Topic B   In this topic, you **modified values** in the query results and saw the values change accordingly in the source table. You also added and removed **fields** in Query Design view. You also learned how to use **Is Null** in the Criteria row to locate null values in a table.

Topic C   In this topic, you used **comparison operators** and separated multiple queries on a field by using the AND and OR conditions. You also used the asterisk (*) **wildcard operator** to view specific text values. You added a **calculated field** to a query by using an expression. You then learned how to use **aggregate functions** to perform calculations on groups of records.

Review questions

1   What is a query?

2   If both queries and filters display data based on selection criteria, how are queries and filters different?

3   When you use the Query Wizard, what information do you need to provide?

4   In which view should you sort a query?

5   Which field criterion is used to find records where no entry has been made in the specific field?

6   Complete the table by filling in the correct comparison operator for the described query.

Description	Operator
Used to specify more than one condition where the query results need to match only one of the conditions.	
Used to specify more than one condition where the query results must match all of the conditions.	
Used as a placeholder when specifying criteria.	

Independent practice activity

In this activity, you'll create and run a query, update data in the query and in its source table, and add a field to the query. Next, you'll create a query that uses comparison operators and the AND condition. You'll change that query to use wildcards. Finally, you'll create a query that uses the Count function.

The files for this activity are in Student Data folder **Unit 5\Unit summary**.

1 Open OrdersIPA.

2 In Design view, create a query, based on the tblOrderItem table, that displays Order ID, ProductID, and Quantity. Run the query.

3 In Datasheet view, modify the query result by changing the value of Quantity for the product with Product ID 5 to **300**.

4 Save the query as **qryPractice**.

5 Verify that the change is reflected in the tblOrderItem table.

6 Add a new field, **curItemPrice**, to the query qryPractice, and run the query.

7 Update and close the query.

8 Create a query based on the tblProduct table that displays all of the product names and unit prices for records having a Unit Price between $1.00 and $2.00. Run the query, and compare your results with Exhibit 5-6.

9 Delete the previous criteria, and display all records where the Product Name begins with **Ce**. Close the query without saving it.

10 Create a query based on the tblOrder table that displays the count of retailers having orders on the same date. (*Hint:* Use Count in the Total row for the field lngOrdRetailerID, and use Group By in the Total row for the field dtmOrddate.) Compare your results with Exhibit 5-7.

11 Close the query without saving.

12 Close the database.

Product Name	Unit Price
Celery Seed (Whole)	$1.75
Celery Seed (Ground)	$1.50
Chives	$1.25
Annatto Seed	$1.23
Cinnamon (Ground) Extra High Oil	$1.99
Asafoetida Powder	$1.49
Anise Seeds	$1.49
Basil Leaf (Whole)	$1.89
Carob Powder (Raw)	$1.89
Basil Leaf (Ground)	$1.45

Exhibit 5-6: The query result after Step 8

CountOfIng(	Order Date
1	5/6/2012
1	5/21/2012
1	6/11/2012
1	6/23/2012
1	7/7/2012
1	8/9/2012
1	8/11/2012
1	9/9/2012
1	9/22/2012
1	10/12/2012
1	11/1/2012
2	1/6/2013
1	1/8/2013
3	2/2/2013
1	2/9/2013
1	3/1/2013
2	3/6/2013
1	4/1/2013

Exhibit 5-7: The query result after Step 10

Unit 6

Using forms

Complete this unit, and you'll know how to:

A Create forms.

B Create and modify forms in Design view.

C Sort and filter records by using forms.

Topic A: Creating forms

This topic covers the following Microsoft Office Specialist exam objectives for Access 2013.

#	Objective
4.1	**Create a Form**
4.1.1	Create new forms
4.1.2	Create forms with application parts
4.1.3	Delete forms
4.3	**Format a Form**
4.3.8	Insert headers and footers

Forms

Explanation

A *form* is an Access database object that allows you to view, edit, and add data to a table. The Datasheet view of a table shows you a grid of fields and rows. A form typically shows just one record at a time. The fields can be arranged on a form and labeled for clarity, as shown in Exhibit 6-1, and they can be made to look like familiar paper documents, such as invoices. The underlying table from which the field values come is referred to as the *source table*. Forms also provide a program interface and can contain buttons and other objects common to other applications. Forms do not need to be connected to any source data.

Form views

There are three views for working with forms:

- **Form view** — The final form as it will be used. See Exhibit 6-1.
- **Layout view** — Looks like Form view, but you can move and format objects.
- **Design view** — The view for building the form, where you add fields and controls and define object properties. See Exhibit 6-2.

Exhibit 6-1: A sample form in Form view

Examining a form in Design view

You can create a form by clicking the Form button on the Create tab on the ribbon or by using the Form Wizard, or you can create a form from scratch in Design view.

To create a form or change its design, you can use Design view, shown in Exhibit 6-2. In Design view, a form contains three main sections:

- **Form Header** — Use this section to enter a heading that describes the form's purpose. This header appears at the top of the form for every record.
- **Detail** — The Detail section contains various controls, such as label and text box controls. Often, the detail section is all you really need.
- **Form Footer** — Use this section to enter information to be displayed at the bottom of a form when it is previewed or printed.

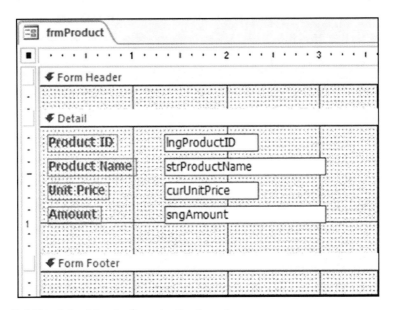

Exhibit 6-2: A basic form in Design view

When you open a form in Design view, three Form Design Tools tabs appear on the ribbon: Design, Arrange, and Format. They are shown in Exhibit 6-3, Exhibit 6-4, and Exhibit 6-5. These tabs contain tools used to add, modify, and arrange controls on the form.

The Form Header and Form Footer sections might not be visible when you open a form in Design view. To show or hide them, right-click the form and choose Form Header/Footer.

Form controls

Every object on an Access form is a control. A *control* displays data, allows you to edit data, or performs some action. Many controls, such as text boxes, list boxes, and option buttons, can link to data in a source table. Other controls, such as labels, shapes, and pictures, are used to make the form clear, organized, and attractive.

The following table describes some of the commonly used controls on the Form Design Tools | Design tab:

Control	Name	Description
Aa	Label	Used to describe the controls used in a form.
ab|	Text Box	Used to enter data such as numbers or text.
◉	Option Button	Used to select a single option from a set of options.
✓	Check Box	Used to select multiple options from a list of options.
	Combo Box	Used to select an option from a drop-down list.
	List Box	Used to select multiple options from a list.

Form Design view can also contain a Field List pane, which shows all of the fields in the table on which the form is based. To display the fields, click the Add Existing Fields button on the Design tab.

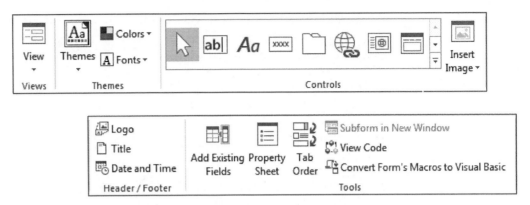

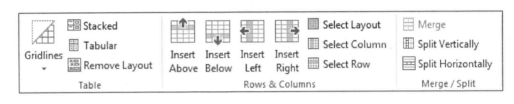

Exhibit 6-3: Tools on the Form Design Tools | Design tab

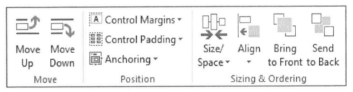

Exhibit 6-4: Tools on the Form Design Tools | Arrange tab

Exhibit 6-5: Tools on the Form Design Tools | Format tab

Do it!

A-1: Examining a form

The files for this activity are in Student Data folder **Unit 6\Topic A**.

Here's how	Here's why
1 Open Transactions1	
2 Open frmProduct in Design view	You'll examine a form. The Form Design Tools—the Design, Arrange, and Format tabs—appear on the ribbon.
3 Right-click a blank area of the form and choose **Form Header/Footer**	To show the Form Header and Form Footer sections.
4 Hide the form header and footer sections	Right-click a blank area of the form and choose Form Header/Footer.
5 Click the **Design** tab	
6 Observe the Controls group	As shown in Exhibit 6-3. It contains controls and other form objects that can be used in forms.
7 Observe the form	The form contains a Detail section. The label controls—such as Product ID, Product Name, Unit Price, and Amount—are on the left side of the window.
8 Observe the text box controls	The field names appear in the text boxes. The form gets the values for these fields from the source table. You can see the values when you switch to Form view.
9 Click **Add Existing Fields**	 Add Existing Fields (In the Tools group.) The Field List pane appears on the right side of the window. It lists the fields you can use on the form.
Click **Add Existing Fields** again	To close the Field List pane.
10 Close the form	Close without saving changes.

Basic forms

Explanation

If you're using the Form button to create a form, all fields in the selected table are automatically included in the form. Here's how to create a form by using this feature:

1   In the Navigation Pane, select a table on which to base the form.
2   Click the Create tab.
3   In the Forms group, click Form.

The new form appears in Layout view. The Form Layout Tools—the Design, Arrange, and Format tabs—appear on the ribbon.

The layout of a form created with the Form button is always columnar. A columnar form displays values in one or more columns, as shown in Exhibit 6-6. A tabular form displays values in a row and column format. After creating a form, you can arrange the controls to better suit your needs.

The form shown in Exhibit 6-6 contains label controls and text box controls. Label controls display the field names, and text box controls display the data in the fields.

Text box controls are an example of *bound controls;* they are linked to the fields of the underlying source table. Any change made in a bound control is reflected in the underlying data source. For example, if you're working in a form and you change data entered in a text box, the underlying field is also changed.

Label controls are an example of *unbound controls;* they are standalone controls that do not have a data source. Other unbound controls are lines, rectangles, and pictures.

Exhibit 6-6: A basic form in Form view

Blank forms

You can create a completely blank form by clicking Blank Form on the Create tab. This will open an empty form and a list of tables and fields that you can drag to it.

The other kind of blank form is one that has a basic layout but is not associated with any data. You can create this kind of blank form by using the Applications Parts feature. On the Create tab, click Application Parts and select a layout under Blank Forms, as shown in Exhibit 6-7. You can then open the form in Design view to edit it.

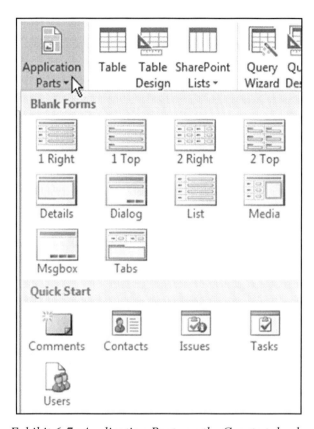

Exhibit 6-7: Application Parts on the Create tab, showing options for blank forms

Do it!   **A-2:   Creating basic and blank forms**

Here's how	Here's why
1 In the Navigation Pane, click **tblRetailer**	To select the underlying source table for the form you will create.
2 Click the **Create** tab	
3 In the Forms group, click **Form**	
	A form opens in Layout view. The Design, Arrange, and Format tabs appear, under Form Layout Tools, on the ribbon.
4 Save the form as **frmBasicForm**	Click the Save button and edit the name. Then click OK to save the form and close the Save As dialog box. The form name appears in the Navigation Pane.
5 Right-click the Form tab and choose **Form View**	To switch to Form view.
Close the form	
6 On the Create tab, click **Application Parts**	
Observe the available templates	Under Blank Forms.
7 Under Blank Forms, click **Details**	To create a blank form. The form name Details appears in the Navigation Pane. This form is not bound to any data.
8 Open the Details form	Double-click it in the Navigation Pane.
Close the form	
9 Delete the Details form	Right-click it in the Navigation Pane and choose Delete. You won't be using this form.

The Form Wizard

Explanation

You can create a form by using the Form Wizard. In the Form Wizard, you can select the fields to be displayed, the order in which they appear, and a layout. The Form Wizard guides you through the steps necessary to create a form. Using the Form Wizard, you can specify which fields you want in the form, whereas creating a basic form with the Form button automatically places all of a table's fields in the form.

To create a form with the Form Wizard:

1 Click the Create tab.

2 In the Forms group, click Form Wizard.

3 Select the table and fields that you want to display in the form. Click Next to move to the next page of the wizard.

4 Select a form layout and click Next.

5 Enter a title for the form and click Finish.

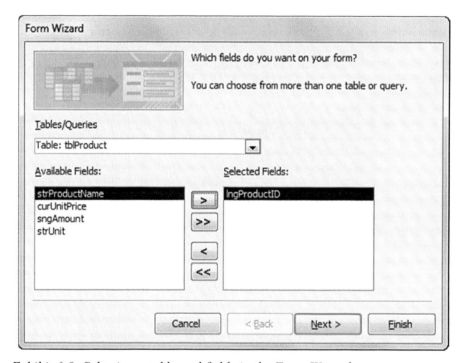

Exhibit 6-8: Selecting a table and fields in the Form Wizard

Do it!   **A-3:   Creating a form by using the Form Wizard**

Here's how	Here's why
1 Click the **Create** tab	
In the Forms group, click **Form Wizard**	To open the Form Wizard.
2 From the Tables/Queries list, select **Table: tblProduct**	To specify the name of the table on which your form will be based. Under Available Fields, all fields of the tblProduct table are listed.
3 Under Available Fields, verify that **lngProductID** is selected	You'll add this field to the Selected Fields list.
Click >	To add lngProductID to the Selected Fields list.
4 Click >>	To add all of the fields to the Selected Fields list.
5 Click **Next**	The wizard now displays form layout options.
6 Verify that **Columnar** is selected	You'll create a form that uses columns.
Click **Next**	
7 Edit the "What title do you want for your form" box to read **frmFormWiz**	This will be the form's title.
Click **Finish**	The form appears in Form view, displaying the first record. The record is shown in a columnar layout.
8 Click ▸	To view the next record in the form.
Click ▸|	To view the last record in the form.
Close the form	The frmFormWiz form is now listed in the Navigation Pane.
9 Close the database	

Topic B: Using Design view

This topic covers the following Microsoft Office Specialist exam objectives for Access 2013.

#	Objective
4.1	**Create a Form**
4.1.1	Create new forms
4.2	**Set Form Controls**
4.2.1	Move form controls
4.2.2	Add form controls
4.2.3	Modify data sources
4.2.4	Remove form controls
4.2.5	Set form control properties
4.2.6	Manage labels
4.3	**Format a Form**
4.3.4	Apply themes
4.3.8	Insert headers and footers

Creating forms in Design view

Explanation

After creating a form, you can open it in Design view. You can add, remove, resize, and rearrange the controls. You can also create a new form from scratch in Design view.

To create a form in Design view:

1   Click the Create tab.
2   In the Forms group, click Form Design.
3   In the Field List, click "Show all tables."
4   In the Field List, expand the table you want to use, and then drag the fields you want to use onto the form.
5   From the Controls group, drag the controls you want to use onto the form.
6   Arrange the controls and set other layout options.
7   Save the form.

You can view one page of a report at a time. In Print Preview, the pointer changes to a magnifying glass so that you can switch between Pages view and Zoom view. In Pages view, one page of a report fits on screen. Zoom view shows an enlarged report.

Outlander Spices
Product Details

Product ID	Product Name	Unit Price	Amount	Unit
1	Cassia	$3.00	2	oz
2	Catnip Leaf	$2.75	2.25	oz
3	Celery Seed (Whole)	$1.75	1	oz
4	Celery Seed (Ground)	$1.50	1	oz
5	Chamomile Flowers	$1.00	2	oz
6	Chili Pepper Powder	$2.00	2.25	oz
7	Chinese Star Anise (G	$3.50	0.5	oz

Exhibit 7-1: The Product Details report in Print Preview

Do it!

A-1: Examining a report

The files for this activity are in Student Data folder **Unit 7\Topic A**.

Here's how	Here's why
1 Open Orders1	
2 Double-click **rptProduct**	To open the report in Print Preview.
3 Point to the report area	The pointer changes to a magnifying glass. You can use it to switch between Pages view and Zoom view.
Click in the report area	To zoom in on the report.
Observe the Preview window	As shown in Exhibit 7-1. It contains both vertical and horizontal scrollbars that you can use to scroll through the report.
4 Observe the headings	The report heading is Outlander Spices Product Details. The field headings include Product ID, Product Name, Unit Price, Amount, and Unit.
Observe the end of the report	(Scroll down.) The current date appears on the left side.
Point anywhere on the report, and click	To zoom out on the report.
5 Close the report	

Basic reports

Explanation

A basic report uses a columnar layout and includes all fields from one table. Here's how to create a basic report:

1   In the Navigation Pane, select the table or query on which you want to base the report.

2   Click the Create tab.

3   In the Reports group, click Report. A columnar report, using all table fields, opens in Layout view.

4   If necessary, use the Design, Arrange, Format, and Page Setup tabs to modify the report in Layout or Design view.

5   Save the new report.

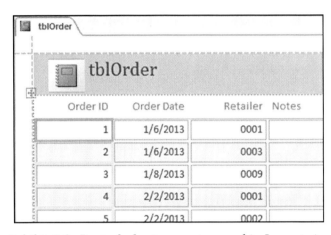

Exhibit 7-2: Part of a basic report opened in Layout view

Blank reports

You can also create a blank report, not based on any table, by clicking the Blank Report button on the Create tab. This will open a blank report and a field list so you can drag fields to the report.

Do it!   **A-2:   Creating blank and basic reports**

Here's how	Here's why
1 Click the **Create** tab	
2 Click **Blank Report**	In the Reports group. This opens a blank report and the Field List pane.
In the Field List pane, click **Show all tables**	(If necessary.) To display a list of tables.
In the Field List pane, click the small **+** to the left of tblOrder	To expand the item and display the fields in tblOrder. You can drag fields from the list to the report.
3 Close the blank report without saving it	You'll create a basic report instead.
4 In the Navigation Pane, select **tblOrder**	You'll base the report on this table.
5 Click the **Create** tab	
In the Reports group, click **Report**	Report
	To create the report and open a preview.
6 Save the report as **rptBasicReport**	It should look like Exhibit 7-2.
7 Click **OK**	To save the report. Its name appears in the Navigation Pane.
8 Close the report	

The Report Wizard

Explanation

When you create a report by using the Report Wizard, you can specify the fields you want to include in the report, and you can arrange the data by specifying a condition for sorting the records. You can also include summary calculations. The Report Wizard guides you through every step of designing a report, from selecting fields to choosing a style for the printed page. The *style* defines the colors and fonts that will be used in the report.

To create a report by using the Report Wizard:

1 Click the Create tab.
2 In the Reports group, click Report Wizard.
3 From the Tables/Queries list, select the table on which the report will be based.
4 In the Available Fields list, select the fields you want to include in the report. Click Next.
5 Select the options you want in the remaining steps of the Report Wizard.
6 Click Finish to exit the wizard and create the report, or click Next to change grouping, sorting, layout, and style options before creating the report.

rptOrderDetails

IngItemOrdID		Product	Detail ID	Quantity	Price Paid	Notes
	1					
		1	1	100	$3.00	
		11	13	50	$4.25	
		12	11	150	$5.50	
	2					
		3	2	400	$1.75	
		7	12	20	$3.50	
	3					
		5	3	200	$1.00	
	4					
		2	4	200	$2.75	
		3	14	200	$1.75	

Exhibit 7-3: Preview of the rptOrderDetails report

Do it! **A-3: Creating a report by using the Report Wizard**

Here's how	Here's why
1 Click the **Create** tab	
In the Reports group, click **Report Wizard**	
2 From the Tables/Queries list, select **Table: tblOrderItem**	You'll create a report based on this table.
3 In the Available Fields list, verify that **lngItemID** is selected	
4 Click >	(The Add button is in the Report Wizard dialog box.) To add lngItemID to the Selected Fields list.
5 Click >>	To add all of the fields. Now all fields appear in the Selected Fields list.
6 Click **Next**	To move to the next page of the Report Wizard.
7 Select **lngItemOrdID**	You'll view records grouped on this field.
8 Click >	To add lngItemOrdID as a grouping level. In the thumbnail, lngItemOrdID appears in a separate box in the top pane. The Grouping Options button is now active.
9 Click **Next**	
Observe the wizard	(The insertion point is in the first list.) You use this page to specify the field by which you want to sort the records in the report.
10 From the first list, select **lngItemProductID**	To sort records by lngItemProductID in ascending order.
11 Click **Next**	To move to the next page of the Report Wizard. The various report layouts appear.
12 Under Layout, verify that **Stepped** is selected	To specify a layout for the report.
Under Orientation, verify that **Portrait** is selected	To specify the orientation of the report.
Verify that **Adjust the field width so all fields fit on a page** is checked	

13	Click **Next**	To move to the next page of the Report Wizard. The available report styles appear.
14	Edit the "What title do you want for your report?" box to read **rptOrderDetails**	To specify the report's title.
	Verify that **Preview the report** is selected	To preview the report on screen before printing it.
	Click **Finish**	You'll see a preview of the report, as shown in Exhibit 7-3. The title of the report is rptOrderDetails. The report shows records from the tblOrderItem table that are grouped by lngItemOrdID and sorted by lngItemProductID.
15	Close the report	
16	Select **rptOrderDetails**	(In the Navigation Pane.) You'll delete this report.
	Press ⌨ DELETE	To delete the report.
	Click **Yes**	To confirm the deletion.

Creating reports in Design view

Explanation

Design view provides you with various tools for designing reports. Tools include the Report Design Tools | Design tab, the Field List pane, and the Property Sheet.

Design view

Report Design view is divided into the following sections: Report Header, Page Header, Group Header, Detail, Group Footer, Page Footer, and Report Footer. These sections control the locations of the report elements. For example, the controls in the Report Header section appear at the beginning of a report. The following table describes each section.

Section	Appears...
Report Header	At the top of the first page of the report. Use this section to show a company logo, the report name, or the date.
Page Header	At the top of every page of the report. It appears below the report header on the first page. Use this section to show the field headings.
Group Header	Before every group of records. A *group* shows records arranged together based on a specific field value. Use this section to display information, such as a group name, that applies to the entire group. For example, you can group records based on products sold to a customer, and the Group Header can contain the name of that customer.
Detail	Once for every record. This section contains the main body of the report and is repeated for each record in the report's source table or query.
Group Footer	At the end of a group of records. Use this section to show information, such as group totals, that is specific to each group.
Page Footer	At the end of every page of the report. Use this section to show information such as page numbers and dates.
Report Footer	At the end of the report, before the page footer on the last page. Use this section to show information such as grand totals.

Interactive controls in reports

Many Access reports are generated to be viewed online. It is possible to make online reports interactive by adding controls like buttons and combo boxes. You can add the same controls to reports that you can add to forms. So, for instance, if you wanted to see reports on individual retailers, you could add a drop-down list of retailers to choose from, and get a report on whichever retailer you selected.

Printed (paper) reports, of course, cannot use interactive features.

Do it!
A-4: Creating a report in Design view

Here's how	Here's why
1 Click the **Create** tab	You'll create a report in Design view.
In the Reports group, click **Report Design**	To open the Design view window. It shows the three default sections of the report: Page Header, Detail, and Page Footer. Four Report Design Tools tabs appear on the ribbon: Design, Arrange, Format, and Page Setup.
2 Drag the Detail bar down as shown	
	To increase the size of the Page Header section.

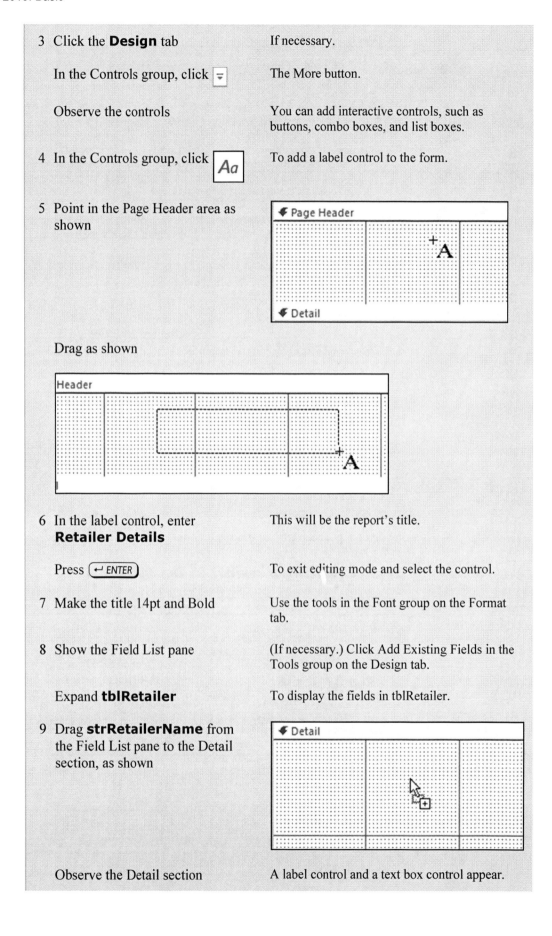

3 Click the **Design** tab — If necessary.

In the Controls group, click ⊽ — The More button.

Observe the controls — You can add interactive controls, such as buttons, combo boxes, and list boxes.

4 In the Controls group, click *Aa* — To add a label control to the form.

5 Point in the Page Header area as shown

Drag as shown

6 In the label control, enter **Retailer Details** — This will be the report's title.

Press ↵ ENTER — To exit editing mode and select the control.

7 Make the title 14pt and Bold — Use the tools in the Font group on the Format tab.

8 Show the Field List pane — (If necessary.) Click Add Existing Fields in the Tools group on the Design tab.

Expand **tblRetailer** — To display the fields in tblRetailer.

9 Drag **strRetailerName** from the Field List pane to the Detail section, as shown

Observe the Detail section — A label control and a text box control appear.

10 Insert other fields as shown	
	Use the Size & Ordering tools on the Arrange tab to align and space the controls. Use the sizing handles to lengthen the name and address fields. Click in the label fields to add a colon (:).
11 On the Design tab, click **Page Numbers**	To open the Page Numbers dialog box.
Under Format, select **Page N of M**	
Under Position, select **Bottom of Page [Footer]**	
Click **OK**	
12 Save the report as **rptRetailerDetails**	
13 Close the Field List pane	Notice that rptRetailerDetails appears in the Navigation Pane.
14 In the Navigation Pane, double-click **rptRetailerDetails**	To view the report.
15 Switch to Print Preview	Click View, Print Preview.
Observe a few pages	The page numbers appear at the bottom.
16 Close the report	
17 Close the database	

Topic B: Modifying and printing reports

This topic covers the following Microsoft Office Specialist exam objectives for Access 2013.

#	Objective
1.3	**Navigate through a Database**
1.3.5	Change views
1.5	**Print and Export a Database**
1.5.1	Print reports
2.3	**Manage Records**
2.3.8	Group records
5.2	**Set Report Controls**
5.2.1	Group data by fields
5.2.2	Sort data
5.3	**Format a Report**
5.3.3	Set margins
5.3.5	Change report orientation
5.3.6	Change sort order
5.3.10	Apply themes

Working in Design and Layout views

Explanation

You can modify a report by using Design view or Layout view. Layout view has the advantage of immed ately showing you how the final report will look. You can do the following:

- Group records based on similar field values.
- Display the sum, average, minimum, and maximum values for each group or for every record.
- Sort or group the data by specific fields in a report.

Moving, resizing, and renaming controls

You can change a report's appearance by changing the properties of the controls and sections in the report. You can also drag a control to a different place and use the sizing handles to resize a control.

Changing the names of controls from their defaults can make it easier to know which is which in the Property Sheet and make it easier to reference the controls programmatically if you ever need to. Give controls names that are descriptive, such as "lblTitle" for the label that holds the report title.

Previewing the report

Print Preview and Report view are similar. Report view is mainly for use on the computer screen, while Print Preview is meant to give you an idea of how the printed report will look. You need to have a printer driver installed to use Print Preview.

Do it!

B-1:   Modifying a report in Design view

The files for this activity are in Student Data folder **Unit 7\Topic B**.

Here's how	Here's why
1 Open Orders2	
2 In the Navigation Pane, double-click **rptOrderItem**	To open the report in Report view.
3 Switch to Print Preview	(Right-click the report tab and select Print Preview, or click the Print Preview button in the status bar.) To see what the printed report will look like. The title isn't centered, and it's not a very helpful title.
4 Switch to Design view	
5 In the Report Header section, change the title qryOrderItem to **Sales Details**	(Select the report heading, click inside the report heading box, and edit it.) To make the report's heading more meaningful.
Select the report heading as shown	
	(Click anywhere outside the report heading, and then select the report heading box.) This is a label control. When you select it, handles appear around the text. Now you can change the size and location of the box.
6 Open the Property Sheet	From the Design tab.
In the Property Sheet, on the Other tab, change the label name to **lblReportTitle**	It is good practice to name controls so that their type and purpose are apparent.
7 Point to the border of the label box, as shown	
	Point to the border, but not to a handle.
Drag the title so it's centered over the fields	Leave the box selected.

8 Change the text color to white	On the Format tab, in the Font group, click the arrow on the Font Color button and select White from the standard colors. The text will be hard to see at first.
Change the report header's Back color to a light shade of blue	Click anywhere in the header section to select it. On the Format tab, in the Font group, click the arrow on the Background Color button and select Light Blue or any other shade of blue.
9 Delete the logo	(To the left of the header.) It was placed there by default when the report was created. Select it and press Delete.
10 In the Detail section, select all four fields	Hold down the Shift key while clicking each field.
In the Font group, click **Center**	(On the Report Layout Tools | Format tab.) To center the data under the headers.
11 Switch to Print Preview	
12 Update and close the report	

Layout view

Explanation   Layout view displays a report just as it would appear on paper. In Layout view, you can move and resize report items and configure the report for printing. You can see the effects of your changes immediately.

Themes

Themes provide a set of default fonts and colors for a report. By using themes, you can ensure that your reports have a consistent look. To use themes, open a report in Design or Layout view and then click Themes. You can see a preview by just pointing to themes in the gallery—your report will temporarily change to the corresponding colors and font styles. To change the colors and fonts separately, use the Colors and Fonts buttons in the Themes group.

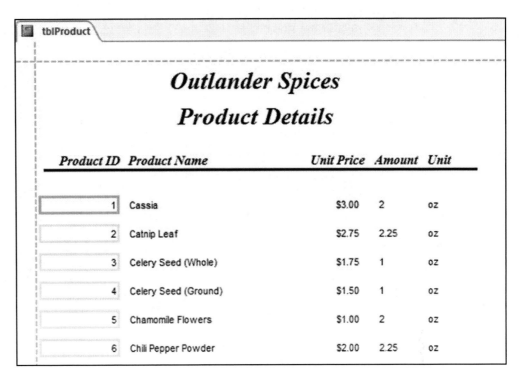

Exhibit 7-4: A report in Layout view

Do it!   **B-2:   Modifying a report in Layout view**

Here's how	Here's why
1 Open rptProduct in Layout view	(Right-click the report name in the Navigation Pane and choose Layout View.) You'll use Layout view to change the design of the report.
Close the Property Sheet	(If necessary.) You won't use it in this activity.
2 Click the first number in the Product ID column	*Product ID* 1 (If necessary.) An orange box highlights the field to indicate that it is selected.
Point to the left side of the field	The pointer changes to a double-headed arrow.
Drag to the right	*Product ID* ↔ 1 Reduce the field to approximately a third of its original size. The Product ID number uses a maximum of four digits, so the field does not have to be large.

3 Drag the **Product ID** field to the right of the Unit field	Amount Unit 2 oz [1] 2.25 oz [2] Point anywhere in the highlighted Product ID field, and drag to the right. The entire column moves to the right side of the report page.
Move the column heading for the Product ID column	Amount Unit │Product ID│ 2 oz 1 2.25 oz 2 Click the column heading to select that field. Point anywhere in the field and drag to the right.
Deselect the field	Click anywhere on the report page.
4 Click the **Product ID** column heading	When you try to select the Product ID heading, the Unit heading is selected instead.
5 Right-click **Unit** and choose **Position, Send to Back**	To move the Unit column heading behind the Product ID column heading.
6 Deselect the Unit heading and then click the **Product ID** column heading again	The field is selected now.
Drag the field to adjust its position relative to the column	If necessary.
7 Update and close the report	
8 Open rptBasicReport in Layout view	
9 On the Design tab, click **Themes**	
Point to different themes in the gallery	(You can scroll down to see more.) The colors and fonts in your report change so you can preview the themes.
Click a theme you like	To apply it to the report. The change is automatically saved.
10 Close the report	

Grouping, sorting, and filtering records in a report

Explanation   You can group records based on a specific field to display records with the same value in that field together. For example, you can group data by Order ID to display all records with the same Order ID together in a report, as shown in Exhibit 7-5. You can place a group name above each group, or place a field showing a total or some other calculated value at the end of each group.

Sales Details

Order ID	Product	Quantity	Price Paid
2	7	20	$3.50
4	34	2	$17.00
5	23	25	$1.23
6	33	4	$14.89
11	29	20	$12.49
11	30	20	$1.89
14	29	10	$12.49
14	25	45	$1.99
16	2	25	$2.75
16	26	10	$1.49
16	4	10	$1.50
28	12	25	$5.50
28	1	25	$3.00
			$79.72

Sales Details

Order ID	Product	Quantity	Price Paid
2			
	7	20	$3.50
4			
	34	2	$17.00
5			
	23	25	$1.23
6			
	33	4	$14.89
11			
	30	20	$1.89
	29	20	$12.49
14			
	25	45	$1.99
	29	10	$12.49
16			
	4	10	$1.50
	26	10	$1.49
	2	25	$2.75
28			
	1	25	$3.00
	12	25	$5.50
			$79.72

Exhibit 7-5: A report sorted by Order ID, and a report sorted and grouped by Order ID.

Grouping and sorting records

To group and sort records, click the Group & Sort button on the Design tab. In the Group, Sort, and Total pane that appears, specify the field and the sort order by which you want to group the records, as shown in Exhibit 7-6.

In the Group, Sort, and Total pane, you can click More to show options for group titles, headers, and footers. If you set any of these, a separate section for Group Header or Group Footer appears in Report Design view. You can use these sections to include information for a group of records.

Exhibit 7-6: The Group, Sort, and Total pane with More options expanded

Filtering

To filter a report, switch to Report view or Layout view. Right-click a field and choose Text Filters or Number Filters, depending on the type of field. Then choose a filter type. Enter the filter criteria and click OK.

Do it!   ### B-3: Grouping, sorting, and filtering a report

Here's how	Here's why
1 Open rptOrderItem in Layout view	You'll use grouping to consolidate report details. Layout view will immediately display the effects of your actions.
2 Click **Group & Sort**	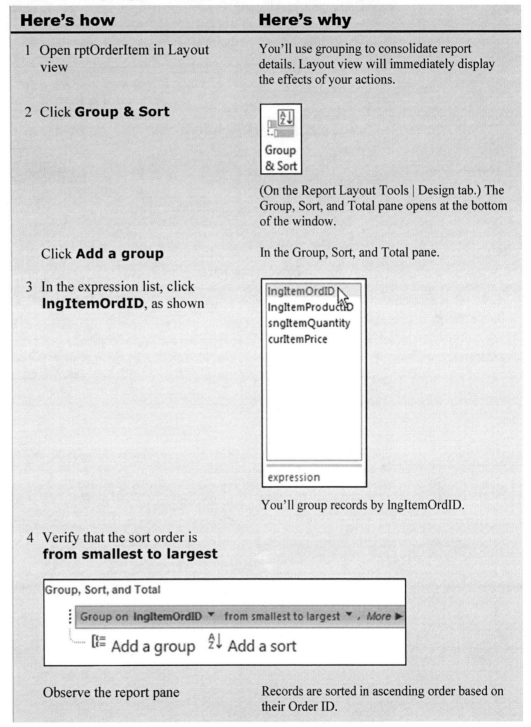 (On the Report Layout Tools | Design tab.) The Group, Sort, and Total pane opens at the bottom of the window.
Click **Add a group**	In the Group, Sort, and Total pane.
3 In the expression list, click **lngItemOrdID**, as shown	lngItemOrdID lngItemProductID sngItemQuantity curItemPrice expression You'll group records by lngItemOrdID.
4 Verify that the sort order is **from smallest to largest**	

Group, Sort, and Total

Group on lngItemOrdID ▼ from smallest to largest ▼ , More ►

[≣ Add a group   ᴬ↓ Add a sort

| Observe the report pane | Records are sorted in ascending order based on their Order ID. |

5 Click the arrow beside "from smallest to largest" and select **from largest to smallest**	from smallest to largest ▾ from smallest to largest from largest to smallest
	To reverse the sort order. The record list is reversed in the report pane.
Close the Group, Sort, and Total pane	
6 Right-click any value in the Quantity field	To display the shortcut menu.
Choose **Number Filters, Greater Than...**	To open the Custom Filter dialog box.
In the box, enter **25**	To filter for those records where the quantity ordered was 25 or greater.
Click **OK**	To close the dialog box and apply the filter.
7 Observe the report	The report displays the details for orders in which the quantity is greater than or equal to 25.
8 Right-click in the Quantity column	
Choose **Clear filter from sngItemQuantity**	To remove the filter.
9 Update and close the report	

Adding summary information

Explanation   Calculated values for groups of records, such as totals and averages, are referred to as *summary operations*. You can add summarized data for a specific field by using either the Report Wizard or Design view.

To add a summary function in a report using the Report Wizard:

1 On the Create tab, click Report Wizard.
2 Select the table or query on which you want to base the report, and add the desired fields. Click Next.
3 Add a field to the grouping level, and click Next.
4 Specify the sort order.
5 Click Summary Options to open the Summary Options dialog box, shown in Exhibit 7-7. Check the summary value you want to calculate.
6 Click OK to close the dialog box and return to the Report Wizard.

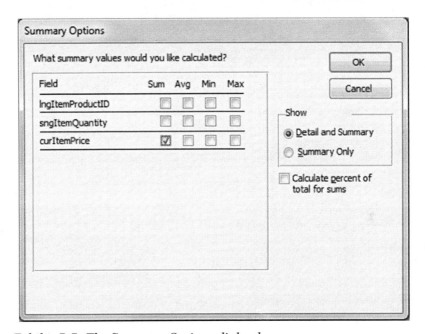

Exhibit 7-7: The Summary Options dialog box

Do it!   **B-4:**   **Adding summary fields with the Report Wizard**

Here's how	Here's why
1 On the Create tab, click **Report Wizard**	In the Reports group.
2 From the Tables/Queries list, select **tblOrderItem**	You'll create a report based on this table.
3 Move the following fields to the Selected Fields list: **lngItemOrdID**, **lngItemProductID**, **sngItemQuantity**, and **curItemPrice**	(Select each field, then click the Add button.) You'll view these fields of the tblOrderItem table in the report.
4 Click **Next**	
Select **lngItemOrdID**	(If necessary.) You'll group records based on this field.
Click ▶	
Click **Next**	To display the next wizard page, on which you can specify the field by which you want to sort the records.
5 From the first list, select **lngItemProductID**	You'll sort records by lngItemProductID.
Click **Summary Options...**	To open the Summary Options dialog box, shown in Exhibit 7-7.
Beside curItemPrice, check **Sum**	To calculate total values for curItemPrice.
Under Show, verify that **Detail and Summary** is selected	
6 Click **OK**	To close the Summary Options dialog box and return to the Report Wizard.
7 Click **Next**	

Report layout and style

Explanation

The arrangement of data and labels in a report is referred to as its *layout*. When you create a report by using the Report Wizard, you can specify a layout and a style instead of using the Report Wizard's default layout and style.

To choose a report layout and style:

1 Select a report layout in the Report Wizard dialog box, as shown in Exhibit 7-8. The default page orientation is Portrait. Click the Landscape button to change the page orientation.
2 Click Next.
3 Select the desired style. Click Next.
4 Enter a title for your report.
5 Click Finish to preview the report.

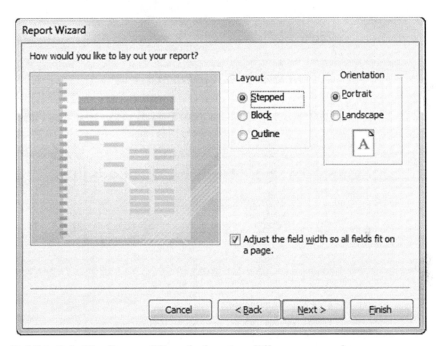

Exhibit 7-8: The Report Wizard, showing different report layouts

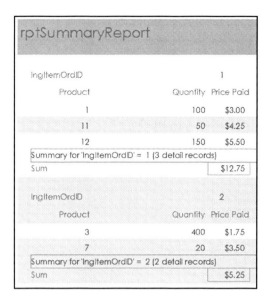

Exhibit 7-9: A layout and style applied to a report

Do it!

B-5: Modifying the layout and style of a report

Here's how	Here's why
1 Verify that the Report Wizard is open	
Observe the wizard	(Shown in Exhibit 7-8.) The current layout, Stepped, is the default layout.
2 Under Layout, select **Outline**	This will be the new report layout.
3 Under Orientation, verify that **Portrait** is selected	
4 Verify that **Adjust the field width so all fields fit on a page** is checked	
5 Click **Next**	
6 Edit the "What title do you want for your report?" box to read **rptSummaryReport**	This will also be the report's name. You can change the title later.
7 Verify that **Preview the report** is selected	
8 Click **Finish**	You'll see a report preview resembling Exhibit 7-9. The total quantity sold to each customer appears in the preview.
9 Close the report	

Printing reports

Explanation   When a report is displayed in Print Preview, the Print Preview tab contains three printing-related groups: Print, Page Size, and Page Layout. (The latter should not be confused with Layout view.) The Page Size and Page Layout groups offer some standard options for paper size, orientation, and margins.

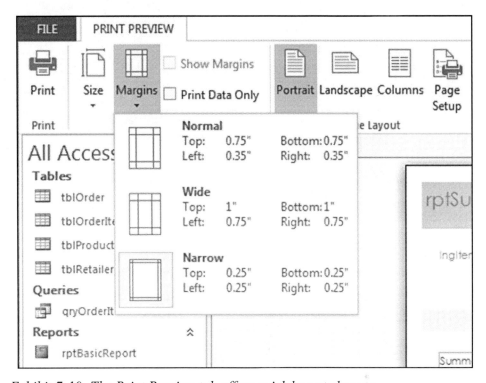

Exhibit 7-10: The Print Preview tab offers quick layout changes

If you need more precise control, the same options found in the Page Size and Page Layout groups can be found in the Page Setup dialog box (shown in Exhibit 7-11), but with text boxes for entering values. Open this dialog box by clicking Page Setup on the Print Preview tab.

Exhibit 7-11: The Page Setup dialog box

If the page setup is correct, you can print the report by clicking the Print button on the Print Preview tab. You can also right-click a report in the Navigation Pane and choose Print. To check printer options before printing, press Ctrl+P to open the Print dialog box. Click OK in this dialog box to send the job to the printer.

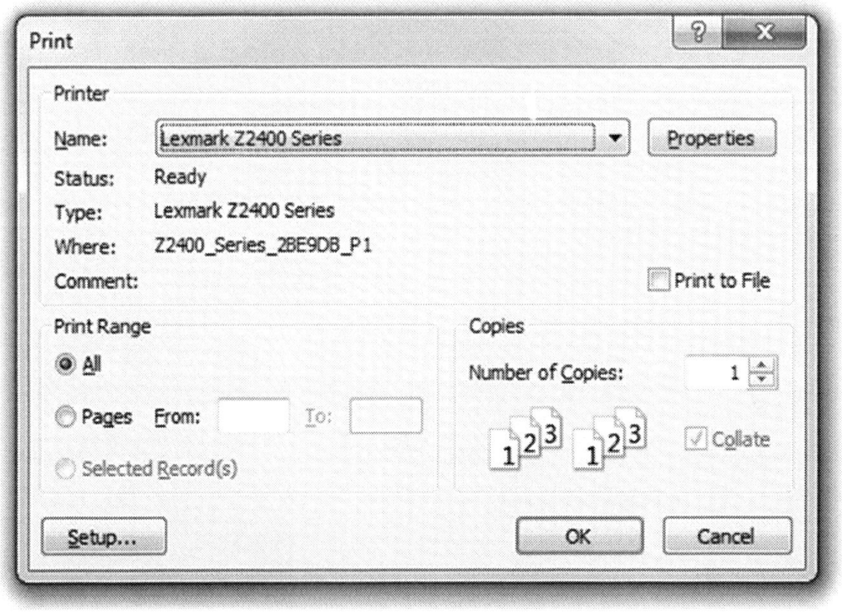

Exhibit 7-12: The Print dialog box

Do it!

B-6:   Printing a report

Here's how	Here's why
1 Open rptSummaryReport in Print Preview mode	You'll review printing and page setup options.
2 In the Page Size group, click **Size** and observe the options	(On the Print Preview tab.) Options include standard paper sizes.
Observe the options for **Margins**	Click the Margins button.
Click **Normal**	To widen the margins.
3 In the Page Layout group, click **Landscape**	The report layout changes to a landscape orientation, with the short edges of the paper on the sides, and the long edges on the top and bottom.
Click **Portrait**	(In the Page Layout group.) To return to a portrait orientation.
4 In the Page Layout group, click **Page Setup**	To open the Page Setup dialog box. It has three tabs: Print Options, Page, and Columns.
Observe the options on each tab	
5 Close the Page Setup dialog box	
6 Click **Print**	 (On the Print Preview tab.) To open the Print dialog box, shown in Exhibit 7-12.
7 Click **Cancel**	To close the Print dialog box.
8 Close the report	
Close the database	

Unit summary: Working with reports

Topic A   In this topic, you created a report by using the **Report button**. You learned that reports created this way automatically contain all fields from the source table. You also created a report by using the **Report Wizard**, which guides you through every step of designing a report. You then created a report in Design view.

Topic B   In this topic, you **modified a report** in Design view and in Layout view. You also **grouped** records and performed summary operations on the records in a report. You selected a style and a **layout** for a report. You also learned how to preview and **print** a report.

Review questions

1   Name any of several ways to create a report.

2   How do you preview a report before printing it?

3   Which of the following is the default layout of a basic report?

   A Columnar   C Portrait

   B Tabular   D Landscape

4   When you are creating a basic report, where do you specify the table or query that contains the source data?

5   What is the procedure to group and sort records in a report?

6   If you want to add total amounts to a report, what feature should you use?

7   Which of the following is not a layout option for a report?

   A Stepped   C Justified

   B Block   D Centered

8 Name one way to print a report.

Independent practice activity

In this activity, you'll create a basic report based on a table. You'll also use the Report Wizard to create and configure a report.

The files for this activity are in Student Data folder **Unit 7\Unit summary**.

1 Open StaffIPA.

2 Create a basic report based on the table tblOrderItem.

3 Save the report as **rptReportPractice** and close the report.

4 Using the Report Wizard, create a report based on the tblEmployee table. Use the following settings:

Item	Setting
Display the fields	lngEmpID, strEmpFirstName, strEmpLastName, strEmpDept, and curEarnings
Group the report by	strEmpDept
Sort in ascending order by	curEarnings
Summarize by calculating the average (Avg) of	curEarnings
Layout	Outline
Specify title	rptEmployeeDetails

5 After previewing the report, center the title, adjust field widths, and center some values to make the report look better. Compare your report with Exhibit 7-13. (*Hint:* Adjust the report in Layout view and Design view.)

6 Preview the report.

7 Update and close the report.

8 Close the database.

9 Close Access.

Employee Details

Department: AC

Earnings	Emp ID	First Name	Last Name
$47,500.00	26	Anna	Morris
$53,500.00	7	Melissa	James
$65,000.00	16	Kendra	James
$76,600.00	2	Shannon	Lee
$80,000.00	25	Pamela	Carter

Avg | $64,520.00 |

Department: AD

Earnings	Emp ID	First Name	Last Name
$30,200.00	3	Melinda	McGregor
$45,000.00	18	Adam	Long
$84,000.00	17	Kevin	Meyers
$87,000.00	4	James	Overmire

Exhibit 7-13: Part of the Employee Details report after Step 5

Appendix A
Microsoft Office Specialist exam objectives

This appendix provides the following information:

A Access 2013 Specialist exam objectives, with references to corresponding coverage in ILT Series courseware.

Topic A: MOS exam objectives

Explanation   The following table lists the Microsoft Office Specialist (MOS) exam objectives for Microsoft Access 2013 and indicates where each objective is covered in conceptual explanations, hands-on activities, or both.

#	Objective	Course level	Conceptual information	Supporting activities
1.0	**Create and Manage a Database**			
1.1	**Create a New Database**			
1.1.1	Create new databases	Basic	Unit 2, Topic A	A-4
1.1.2	Create databases use templates	Basic	Unit 2, Topic A	A-2
1.1.3	Create databases in older formats	Advanced	Unit 6, Topic A	A-1
1.1.4	Create databases use wizards	Basic	Unit 7, Topic A	A-3
1.2	**Manage Relationships and Keys**			
1.2.1	Edit references between tables	Intermediate	Unit 1, Topic C	C-1
1.2.2	Create and modify relationships	Intermediate	Unit 1, Topic B	B-2
1.2.3	Set primary key fields	Basic	Unit 2, Topic C	C-4, C-8
1.2.4	Enforce referential integrity	Intermediate	Unit 1, Topic C	C-2
1.2.5	Set foreign keys	Intermediate	Unit 1, Topic B	B-1
1.2.6	View relationships	Intermediate	Unit 1, Topic C	C-1
1.3	**Navigate through a Database**			
1.3.1	Navigate to specific records	Basic	Unit 3, Topic B	B-1
1.3.2	Set a form as the startup option	Intermediate	Unit 4, Topic E	E-5
1.3.3	Use navigation forms	Intermediate	Unit 4, Topic E	E-5
1.3.4	Set navigation options	Basic	Unit 1, Topic B	B-3
1.3.5	Change views	Basic	Unit 2, Topic B	B-4
1.4	**Protect and Maintain a Database**			
1.4.1	Compact databases	Advanced	Unit 6, Topic A	A-4
1.4.2	Repair databases	Advanced	Unit 6, Topic A	A-4
1.4.3	Back up databases	Advanced	Unit 6, Topic A	A-5
1.4.4	Split databases	Advanced	Unit 6, Topic A	A-3

#	Objective	Course level	Conceptual information	Supporting activities
1.4	**Protect and Maintain a Database (continued)**			
1.4.5	Encrypt databases with a password	Advanced	Unit 6, Topic B	B-1
1.4.6	Merge databases	Advanced	Unit 5, Topic A	A-1
1.4.7	Recover data from backups	Advanced	Unit 6, Topic A	A-5
1.5	**Print and Export a Database**			
1.5.1	Print reports	Basic	Unit 7, Topic B	B-6
1.5.2	Print records	Intermediate	Unit 5, Topic C	C-1
1.5.3	Maintain backward compatibility	Advanced	Unit 6, Topic A	A-1
1.5.4	Save databases as templates	Basic	Unit 2, Topic A	A-3
1.5.5	Save databases to external locations	Advanced	Unit 6, Topic A	A-5
1.5.6	Export to alternate formats	Advanced	Unit 5, Topic B	B-4

2.0 Build Tables

#	Objective	Course level	Conceptual information	Supporting activities
2.1	**Create a Table**			
2.1.1	Create new tables	Basic	Unit 2, Topic C	C-2
2.1.2	Import External data into tables	Advanced	Unit 5, Topic A	A-2
2.1.3	Create linked tables from external sources	Advanced	Unit 5, Topic D	D-1
2.1.4	Import tables from other database	Advanced	Unit 5, Topic A	A-4
2.1.5	Create tables from templates and application parts	Basic	Unit 2, Topic C	C-1
2.2	**Format a Table**			
2.2.1	Hide fields in tables	Basic	Unit 3, Topic B	B-3
2.2.2	Change data formats	Basic	Unit 4, Topic A	A-6
2.2.3	Add total rows	Basic	Unit 3, Topic A	A-5
2.2.4	Add table descriptions	Basic	Unit 2, Topic C	C-1, C-3
2.2.5	Rename tables	Basic	Unit 2, Topic C	C-1, C-7

#	Objective	Course level	Conceptual information	Supporting activities
2.3	**Manage Records**			
2.3.1	Update records	Basic	Unit 3, Topic B	B-1
2.3.2	Add new records	Basic	Unit 2, Topic C	C-6
2.3.3	Delete records	Basic	Unit 3, Topic C	C-7
2.3.4	Append records from external data	Advanced	Unit 5, Topic A	A-5
2.3.5	Find and replace data	Basic	Unit 3, Topic B	B-1
2.3.6	Sort records	Basic	Unit 3, Topic B	C-1
2.3.7	Filter records	Basic	Unit 3, Topic B	C-1
2.3.8	Group records	Basic	Unit 7, Topic B	B-3
2.4	**Create and Modify Fields**			
2.4.1	Add fields to tables	Basic	Unit 2, Topic C	C-3
			Unit 3, Topic A	A-2
2.4.2	Add validation rules to tables	Basic	Unit 4, Topic C	C-1
2.4.3	Change field captions	Basic	Unit 3, Topic A	A-2
2.4.4	Change field sizes	Basic	Unit 4, Topic A	A-3
2.4.5	Change field data types	Basic	Unit 2, Topic C	C-3
2.4.6	Configure fields to auto-increment	Basic	Unit 2, Topic C	C-3
2.4.7	Set default values	Basic	Unit 4, Topic A	A-5
2.4.8	Use input masks	Basic	Unit 4, Topic B	B-1
2.49	Delete fields	Basic	Unit 3, Topic A	A-2

3.0   Create Queries

3.1   Create a Query

#	Objective	Course level	Conceptual information	Supporting activities
3.1.1	Run queries	Basic	Unit 5, Topic A	A-4
3.1.2	Create crosstab queries	Advanced	Unit 2, Topic A	A-2
3.1.3	Create parameter queries	Advanced	Unit 2, Topic B	B-1
3.1.4	Create action queries	Basic	Unit 5, Topic A	A-3
3.1.5	Create multi-table queries	Intermediate	Unit 3, Topic A	A-2
3.1.6	Save queries	Basic	Unit 5, Topic A	A-4
3.1.7	Delete queries	Advanced	Unit 2, Topic C	C-2

#	Objective	Course level	Conceptual information	Supporting activities
3.2	**Modify a Query**			
3.2.1	Rename queries	Advanced	Unit 2, Topic C	C-4
3.2.2	Add new fields	Basic	Unit 5, Topic B	B-2
3.2.3	Remove fields	Basic	Unit 5, Topic B	B-2
3.2.4	Hide fields	Basic	Unit 5, Topic B	B-2
3.2.5	Sort data within queries	Basic	Unit 5, Topic A	A-5
3.2.6	Format fields within queries	Intermediate	Unit 3, Topic B	B-2
3.3	**Utilize Calculated Fields and Grouping within a Query**			
3.3.1	Add calculated fields	Intermediate	Unit 3, Topic B	B-1
3.3.2	Add conditional logic	Intermediate	Unit 3, Topic B	B-3
3.3.3	Group and summarize data	Basic	Unit 5, Topic C	C-6
3.3.4	Use comparison operators	Basic	Unit 5, Topic C	C-1
3.3.5	Use basic operators	Basic	Unit 5, Topic C	C-3
4.0	**Create Forms**			
4.1	**Create a Form**			
4.1.1	Create new forms	Basic	Unit 6, Topic A	A-2
4.1.2	Create forms with application parts	Basic	Unit 6, Topic A	A-2
4.1.3	Delete forms	Basic	Unit 6, Topic A	A-2
4.2	**Set Form Controls**			
4.2.1	Move form controls	Basic	Unit 6, Topic B	B-2
4.2.2	Add form controls	Basic	Unit 6, Topic B	B-2
4.2.3	Modify data sources	Basic	Unit 6, Topic B	B-2
4.2.4	Remove form controls	Basic	Unit 6, Topic B	B-2
4.2.5	Set form control properties	Basic	Unit 6, Topic B	B-3
4.2.6	Manage labels	Basic	Unit 6, Topic B	B-2

#	Objective	Course level	Conceptual information	Supporting activities
4.3	**Format a Form**			
4.3.1	Modify tab order in forms	Intermediate	Unit 4, Topic A	A-2
4.3.2	Format print layouts	Intermediate	Unit 4, Topic A	A-5
4.3.3	Sort records	Basic	Unit 6, Topic C	C-1
4.3.4	Apply themes	Basic	Unit 6, Topic B	B-3
4.3.5	Change margins	Intermediate	Unit 4, Topic A	A-5
4.3.6	Insert backgrounds	Intermediate	Unit 4, Topic B	B-3
4.3.7	Auto-order forms	Intermediate	Unit 4, Topic A	A-2
4.3.8	Insert headers and footers	Basic	Unit 6, Topic B	B-1
4.3.9	Insert images	Intermediate	Unit 4, Topic B	B-1
4.3.10	Modify existing forms	Intermediate	Unit 4, Topic D	D-1

5.0   Create Reports

5.1   Create a Report

#	Objective	Course level	Conceptual information	Supporting activities
5.1.1	Create new reports	Basic	Unit 7, Topic A	A-2
5.1.2	Create reports with application parts	Intermediate	Unit 5, Topic A	A-9
5.1.3	Delete reports	Basic	Unit 7, Topic A	A-3
5.2	**Set Report Controls**			
5.2.1	Group data by fields	Basic	Unit 7, Topic B	B-3
5.2.2	Sort data	Basic	Unit 7, Topic B	B-3
5.2.3	Add subreports	Intermediate	Unit 5, Topic D	B-3
5.2.4	Modify data sources	Basic	Unit 7, Topic A	A-4
5.2.5	Add report controls	Basic	Unit 7, Topic A	A-4
5.2.6	Manage labels	Basic	Unit 7, Topic A	A-4
5.3	**Format a Report**			
5.3.1	Format reports into multiple columns	Intermediate	Unit 5, Topic A	A-7
5.3.2	Add calculated fields	Intermediate	Unit 5, Topic B	B-1
5.3.3	Set margins	Basic	Unit 7, Topic B	B-6
5.3.4	Add backgrounds	Intermediate	Unit 5, Topic D	A-8

#	Objective	Course level	Conceptual information	Supporting activities
5.3	**Format a Report (continued)**			
5.3.5	Change report orientation	Basic	Unit 7, Topic B	B-6
5.3.6	Change sort order	Basic	Unit 7, Topic B	B-3
5.3.7	Insert headers and footers	Intermediate	Unit 5, Topic A	A-1, A-2
5.3.8	Insert images	Intermediate	Unit 5, Topic A	A-1
5.3.9	Insert page numbers	Basic	Unit 7, Topic A	A-4
5.3.10	Apply themes	Basic	Unit 7, Topic B	B-2
5.3.11	Modify existing reports	Intermediate	Unit 5, Topic A	A-1

Course summary

This summary contains information to help you bring the course to a successful conclusion. Using this information, you will be able to:

A Use the summary text to reinforce what you've learned in class.

B Determine the next courses in this series, as well as any other resources that might help you continue to learn about Microsoft Access.

Topic A: Course summary

Use the following summary text to reinforce what you've learned in class.

Unit summaries

Unit 1

In this unit, you learned that a **database** is used to store data in tables. You also learned about fields and records. Next, you learned how to start Access, and you examined the **Access window**. Finally, you opened a database with shared access and examined the **database window**.

Unit 2

In this unit, you learned how to **create a database** by using the database templates. You also learned about Datasheet and Design views for tables. Next, you **created a table** by using table templates and Design view. You also learned how to set the **primary key** and **add fields** in a table. Then, you learned how to save a table and add records to it. Next, you learned how to copy, rename, and delete tables. Finally, you learned how to create a **composite key** and use the Data Type gallery.

Unit 3

In this unit, you learned how to **modify a table** by changing field names and deleting, inserting, and moving fields. Then, you learned how to use the **Attachment** data type. You also learned how to add a **Totals row** to a table. Next, you learned how to use the **Find and Replace** dialog box. You also learned how to undo changes in a table. Finally, you learned how to **sort** and **filter** records in a table.

Unit 4

In this unit, you learned how to set the Required, Allow Zero Length, Field Size, Append Only, and Default Value **field properties**. Next, you learned how to set **input masks** for fields. Then you learned how to set Validation Text and **Validation Rule** properties for a field.

Unit 5

In this unit, you learned how to plan and create a **query**. You created queries by using the Query Wizard and Design view. You also learned how to **sort** and **filter** records in query results. Next, you modified the values in a query result. Finally, you learned how to use **comparison operators**, **calculated fields**, and **aggregate functions** in a query.

Unit 6

In this unit, you learned how to create a **form** by using the Form Wizard. Then you learned how to create a form in Design view, **add controls**, and modify the properties of controls, including through the use of **conditional formatting**. Finally, you learned how to use forms to **sort** and **filter** records.

Unit 7

In this unit, you learned how to create a basic **report** by using the Report button. You also created reports by using the Report Wizard, Design view, and Layout view. You then learned how to **group records** and **add summary information** in reports. Finally, you learned how to select a report layout and **print** a report.

Topic B: Continued learning after class

It is impossible to learn how to use any software effectively in a single day. To get the most out of this class, you should begin working with Access to perform real tasks as soon as possible. We also offer resources for continued learning.

Next courses in this series

This is the first course in this series. The next courses in this series are:

- *Access 2010: Intermediate*
- *Access 2010: Advanced*

Other resources

For more information on this and other topics, go to **www.Crisp360.com**.

Crisp360 is an online community where you can expand your knowledge base, connect with other professionals, and purchase individual training solutions.

Glossary

Aggregate function

A function that calculates values for a group of records by adding the values to the Totals row of the query design grid.

Allow Zero Length property

A property that specifies that the field can contain null values.

AND comparison operator

An operator that specifies more than one condition in the criteria and displays the records that satisfy all of the conditions.

Append Only property

A property that specifies that a memo field can be added to by users, but users cannot delete or change field data.

Bound controls

Controls that are linked to the fields of the underlying source table. Any change made in a bound control is reflected in the underlying data source. Text box controls are an example of bound controls.

Comparison operators

Operators that add criteria to a query so you can view records based on multiple conditions.

Composite key

A primary key that uses two fields. Composite keys are typically used if a table has no single field that can serve as the primary key. Also called a compound key or a multi-field key.

Control

An object in a form that displays data, allows users to edit data, or performs some action.

Data value

An item of data.

Database

An organized collection of information. An example of a simple database is a phone book that contains the names, phone numbers, and addresses of individuals and businesses.

Database management program

An application that stores and organizes data and makes data retrieval efficient.

Datasheet view

An Access view that displays data in a tabular format, with rows and columns. Use Datasheet view to scroll through records and add, edit, or view data in a table.

DefaultValue property

A property that assigns a default value for a field, even if nothing is entered in the field.

Design view

A view that gives users complete control over the structure of a table, form, query, or report.

Entity

Any object that has a distinct set of properties.

Expression

A combination of symbols—identifiers, operators, and values—that produces a result. An expression can include the normal arithmetic operators for addition (+), subtraction (-), multiplication (*), and division (/).

Field

A specific type of information that applies to all items listed in a table.

Field Size property

A property that specifies the maximum number of characters that can be entered in the field.

File format

The specific format in which each application stores data. By default, Access 2010 creates databases in the Access 2007 file format.

Filter

A set of conditions applied to data in order to show just a subset of it.

Filtering

The process of temporarily isolating a subset of records that satisfy certain criteria you specify.

Form

An Access database object that allows users to view, edit, and add data to a table. The Datasheet view of a table shows a grid of fields and rows, while a form typically shows just one record at a time.

Form Wizard

A form-creation tool that prompts users to select the fields to be included, the order in which the fields will appear, and a layout for the form.

Format property

A property that specifies the display format for data in a field.

Group

A feature that organizes database objects through shortcuts.

Handles

Small, black rectangles around a control; used to change the size and position of a control.

Input mask

A feature used to define how data should be entered in a field. Also determines the type of data and the number of characters that can be entered in the field.

Input Mask Wizard

A tool used to create an input mask based on the built-in input masks in Access.

Layout

The arrangement of data and labels in a report.

Macro

A set of commands used to automate frequently performed database tasks, such as printing a set of weekly reports.

Module

A program that automates and customizes database operations. Modules are written in Visual Basic.

Navigation Pane

The left pane of the Database window. It lists various database objects, such as tables, forms, and queries.

Null value

A value that indicates missing or unknown data in a field.

OLE Object data type

A type of data that links to objects created in other applications, such as Microsoft Word.

OR comparison operator

An operator that specifies two conditions in the criteria and displays the records that satisfy either of these conditions.

PivotChart view

A table view used to display data graphically.

PivotTable view

A table view used to analyze data.

Primary key

A field that uniquely identifies each record in a table.

Property Sheet

A pane used to change the properties of a form, table, query, or report. A Property Sheet contains five tabs: Format, Data, Event, Other, and All.

Query

A database object that retrieves data based on criteria from one or more tables and displays it.

Record

A single set of related data values.

Record selector

The small box to the left of each record in a table; used to navigate through the records. The record selector points to the active record and indicates its status.

Relational database

A type of database in which data is organized in the form of related tables. In related tables, one or more fields are linked to fields in another table. This link ensures that users can enter only those values that have corresponding entries in the other table.

Report

An Access database object that presents data in an organized format suitable for viewing on screen or printing.

Report Wizard

A report-creation tool that prompts users to select the fields they want to include.

Required property

A property that specifies that a field cannot contain null values. If the Required property is set to Yes, a value must be entered in the field.

Row selector

An interface element that uses a black triangle to indicate the active row in Design view.

Sorting

The process of organizing records in a meaningful way so that users can retrieve data in the order they wish.

Source table

The underlying table containing the data that provides the field values in a form.

Summary operations

Calculated values, such as totals and averages, for groups of records. Users can add summarized data for a specific field by using the Report Wizard or Design view.

Table

A database object that consists of a collection of records that store data.

Template
A predefined database structure or table structure provided by Access or created by a user.

Unbound controls
Standalone controls that do not have a data source. Use unbound controls to display labels, lines, rectangles, and pictures.

Validation rule
A rule used to verify that data matches the conditions specified for the type of data, the data format, or the number of characters that can be entered in a field.

Validation Text property
A property used to define the error message that is displayed when the validation rule is not satisfied.

Wildcard operators
Placeholders that specify criteria in query conditions to retrieve multiple values There are two frequently used wildcard operators: the question mark (?) and the asterisk (*). The question mark is used to substitute for a single character. The asterisk is used to substitute for any number of characters.

Index